Volume Cycles in the Stock Market

Market Timing through Equivolume Charting

RICHARD W. ARMS, JR.

ISBN 1-885439-00-8

Printed in the United States of America

Preface

When *Profits in Volume,* my first book on the stock market, was written, my intention was to present in a simple manner a new way of depicting stock action. *Equivolume Charting* was to be a better way of seeing what was happening to stock prices and stock volume, and was intended to utilize the many accepted principles of technical analysis, adapting them to the new charting method.

Even as its inventor, I did not realize for some time the magnitude of the concept. The abandoning of time in favor of volume as a market yardstick carried implications which only emerged slowly, and as they emerged they brought a new logic to the marketplace. Apparent randomness gave way to predictability as it became obvious that the market had rhythms as dependable as the ebb and flow of the tides.

Many of the traditional methods of technical analysis had to be abandoned, so a search was begun for better analytical techniques which could incorporate the nontime concept. This book contains the results of that search.

I would ask the reader to set aside, at least temporarily, his prior training in technical analysis and open his mind to the volume concept. Accept the premise that stocks live in their own world, a world that is not governed by wristwatches and calendars, but by trading.

Understanding these new concepts of *volume cyclicality,* and *ease of movement* requires a basic understanding of Equivolume charts. Consequently, the first section of this book contains a review of this analytical technique, the construction of Equivolume charts, and their interpretation.

After reintroducing Equivolume Charting, we will stand way back and observe the rhythmic music of the market. We will see how the opposing emotions fear and greed are translated into supply and demand, whereupon they push and pull prices producing predictable tides, waves, and ripples.

Next, we will look at the same data with a microscope, dissecting each entry, giving them numerical values and weighing the importance of those values, and then arriving at a ranking for each entry, which we will call ease of movement value.

Finally, we will combine everything we have been able to learn into a reliable technique of market trading, a nonemotional, business-like discipline with the sole purpose of making profits.

ACKNOWLEDGMENTS   Putting a book together, especially while meeting a deadline, calls for a very understanding wife and family. I am especially fortunate that my wife, June, not only suffered through this but also helped by listening to chapter after chapter and lending many helpful suggestions. Even more valuable was her artistic talent, which was utilized in the preparation of graphics as well as in the Rubaiyat illustration at the beginning of the book.

Debbie Cummings, whose job was to be a typist, ended up as a valuable critic and a devoted assistant.

Dr. and Mrs. David Johnson were invaluable in reading copy and making suggestions, as were Ben Raskob and Bob Hickman.

My thanks to all these people for their help.

Contents

Foreword

My personal dream is a simple one: to create tools which help people become more successful computerized investors. But I know from my own trading experience that successful investing involves more than just using analysis tools. There is also the educational aspect, where we all acquire a deeper understanding of methodologies.

That is why we are pleased to offer you this book as part of the EQUIS University program. In *Volume Cycles of the Stock Market*, Dick Arms not only describes the popular equivolume studies he developed, but also explains how they can be applied in a practical way.

With the inclusion of Dick's methodologies into MetaStock™, we are now able to provide a more comprehensive implementation of Equivolume than has ever been made available to computerized investors. We hope you benefit from Dick's techniques as much as we know others have.

> Steven B. Achelis
> President/CEO
> EQUIS International, Inc.

Introduction

There is only one reason to buy a stock—to make money. There are other investments that provide a higher income and do it with more safety, so just dividends do not justify the buying of stocks. Stocks are supposed to be an inflation hedge, but recent history has not justified this either.

The wonderful thing about stocks is that they go up and down quite rapidly and quite predictably. It is this movement that makes them attractive as a way of making money. But making money in stocks is not easy. It takes knowledge and discipline and hard work. Today's market is dominated by professionals—money managers whose job it is to invest funds intelligently. Theirs is a full-time job, and their jobs depend upon results. To be successful, the individual investor must be as professional, as detached, as systematic as these professionals. Such professionalism and such discipline necessitate a plan—a methodology. This book contains such a plan.

In the pages that follow, the reader will be led through a unique system of technical analysis. No mention will ever be made of price-earnings ratios, cash flow, dividends, growth rates, or profit margins. In fact, all fundamental factors will be completely ignored since they appear to have so little bearing on stock prices. Rather, we will learn to listen to the market in its own voice, a voice which speaks to us in terms of price and volume. We will allow this communication, directly from the market, to help us to make our decisions.

Our interest is going to be when, not what. A company may, due to the balancing of supply and demand for its stock, trade at $50 per share or $30 per share, yet it is the same company with little change in any fundamentals. The only difference is in people's desire to own the stock. We are interested in knowing the points at which demand is overcoming supply and forcing prices upward or supply is overcoming demand and forcing prices downward. Price and volume figures can relay this information.

It is our contention that volume is the most important, the least understood, and the most ignored factor in the marketplace. Prices only move because of trading, which is volume, and the way in which they move is a function of volume.

Time, the normal way of evaluating the market, is a human measurement, whereas volume is a market measurement. Without trading, nothing happens, regardless of how much time goes by. If the market were to wear a wristwatch, its dial would be divided into shares instead of minutes and hours. We will study these volume figures, relate them to prices, and attempt to arrive at a useful system for buying and selling stocks.

Those readers who are familiar with the author's earlier writings may want to skip the first part of this book, which reviews those earlier publications. However, experience and further study have led to a few changes, especially in the use of trend lines, and we suggest at least a quick glance through Part One.

The balance of the book contains totally new ideas, using the original work as a foundation. The book, as a whole, contains a complete method of stock market analysis, designed to stand alone without reliance on other methods. It should be used in that way, rather than being treated as an additional tool to be merged with other methods. We believe a thorough knowledge of the techniques which follow, and a careful application of those techniques, can lead the reader to the one objective in buying stocks—*profits!*

Part One   Equivolume Charting

Chapter 1   Volume—The Market Measure

The stock market is just opening on Monday morning. A broker with some stock to sell enters the trading crowd for American Telephone and sells 5,000 shares at a quarter of a point less than Friday's closing price. The stock is down only slightly, but in that single trade over $215 million are lost, at least on paper. That small move evokes an emotional response. Every holder of American Telephone, whatever it may be—10 shares or 100,000 shares—feels the loss and reacts with a slight twinge of fear. Additionally, every person who would like to own the stock, but does not, has a slight increase in that desire, a feeling that the stock is now just slightly cheaper and that maybe it is time to buy.

Price moves bring about emotional feelings in us, be they slight or great. Fear and greed, the two powerful forces which govern all stock market activity, are primarily a result of prices and their movement.

In reality, of course, the quarter-point move was effected by the sale of only 5,000 shares even though it caused the reevaluation of all of the 861,981,000 shares of American Telephone stock outstanding. But it was the price move, not the number of shares, which slightly nudged people's emotions all around the world. Five thousand shares is not a large trade, and the next few trades could easily recoup the drop in a matter of seconds, but every move causes an emotional reaction.

Every time a transaction between a buyer and a seller takes place, two significant pieces of information are generated, yet we tend to react emotionally to one and largely ignore the other. Price changes can bring about elation or depression, but volume usually elicits only a yawn. Yet volume is perhaps the most valuable tool available to the market participants. Whereas price tells us *what* is happening, volume tells us *how* it is happening, and that how may mean the difference between success and failure.

A stock which moves up three points in a day on light volume is telling a far different story from one moving up the same amount on very heavy volume. A stock which normally has low volume may suddenly trade very heavy volume, but make little progress. It is telling an entirely different story. Increasing or decreasing volume after an extended upward move are each divulging information—yet entirely different information. Only by understanding volume can we correctly interpret the price moves we see. To ignore volume is to enter the boxing ring with a patch over one eye. We are dealing with money, money that is important to us. We cannot afford to have a blind side. We must use every faculty available to us or a fist may swing at us from that blind side and knock us out of the ring.

In a single trade, as in the 5,000 shares of American Telephone, we are only seeing price and volume. At the end of the day a third piece of information is also derived. That information is the *price spread*. The price spread is the measure of the distance between the highest price the stock traded during the day and the lowest price it traded during the same day. If, for example, a stock had a high today of 55⅞ and a low of 54⅞, it would have a spread of one point. During the day, it may have had a number of upward and downward moves, but these moves were confined within the 54⅞–55⅞ limits. The price range is, in itself, imparting valuable information. We know that the stock couldn't seem to get above 55⅞ without encountering sellers, nor could it decline below 54⅞ without meeting buyers willing to hold the price up. A wide price spread would indicate a large disagreement between buyers and sellers as to the value of the stock. A narrow price spread would indicate that buyers and sellers are more in agreement, at least for the present.

Let us then look back at the rest of the information, the forgotten factor of volume, and see how it relates to price spread. The price spread has told us what has happened, but the volume can tell us *how* it happened. By studying both the price spread and the volume, we get a picture of how easy or hard it is for the stock to move. A stock with a small price spread and low volume would indicate nothing more than a general lack of interest. There is little difference between the high and the low because of apathy, and that apathy is made apparent by the light trading. Nobody is particularly interested in either buying or selling the stock. If, on the other hand, very heavy trading (as compared to the usual volume for this particular stock) takes place while the trading range is comparatively small, there is a sharp disagreement between stubborn sellers and stubborn buyers. The sellers will not let the stock go up, the buyers will not let it go down, and both groups are exerting a large amount of pressure. That pressure is the volume. There are large numbers of shares represented on both sides. It is somewhat like trench warfare. The aggressors and the defenders are firmly dug in, and there is heavy hand-to-hand combat. But neither army can penetrate the other's lines.

Let us now consider a stock with a comparatively large trading spread. We use the word *comparatively* because our judgment of each price spread must, in fact, be a comparison to what would be considered a normal or average spread for that particular stock. (More about this in later chapters.) Our wide spread would indicate that there is less reluctance for the stock to move. Going back to our prior analogy, the trenches are not as close together, and the warfare consists of artillery and sniping rather than bayonets. The volume can tell us a lot more at this point also. Generally, wide price spreads are seen when prices are advancing or declining. One of our two armies is falling back while the other is attacking. Volume tells us how much resistance the attackers are encountering. Heavy volume tells us that it is taking a powerful attack to move the defenders back, while lighter volume is indicative of a rout.

We do see wider price ranges which do not accompany an important price move, but they are less common. When it happens, volume again helps to tell us how it is happening. A light volume indicates a backing away by the public. Neither buyers nor sellers are very sure of themselves, and a vacuum seems to exist between them. Prices can move easily between two widely separated extremes. It is a period of indecision. The armies are lobbing occasional mortar rounds at one another, and neither is launching an attack.

If we see heavy trading with a wide price spread and our stock is not in a significant advance or decline, the indecision is still there, but both sides are becoming very active. They are both trying to break down each other's defenses prior to a major battle. Typically, we would expect the battle lines to close, hand-to-hand combat to begin and then one army to drive the other from their trenches.

As we have seen in the prior examples, volume is the key to understanding stock action. It is the second term in the equation, an often ignored term, but a necessary one if the result is to be useful. Prior to the advent of Equivolume Charting in 1971, there was no good graphic way of working with volume. It was relegated to a secondary position, almost an afterthought, along the lower margins of vertical line (bar) charts, or completely omitted, as in point-and-figure charts. Equivolume changed that by moving it to its proper position as an equal partner with price. In the following six chapters, we will review and, in a few ways, revise the methods of constructing and interpreting Equivolume charts.

Chapter 2   Constructing Equivolume Charts

If, as we have suggested, volume figures should be offered a full partnership with price figures, rather than the menial job of creeping along the lower margin of a bar chart, we need a graphic method of doing this. The graphic method is known as Equivolume charting. In its construction, it consists only of moving the volume information off the bottom of the chart and including it in the price postings.

Let us look at a typical vertical line or bar chart (take your pick on names) and review its construction (Figure 2–1). We see that the upper vertical scale is price while the horizontal scale is time. The major price divisions are dollar prices per share and are subdivided into eighths, since stocks normally are priced in eighths of a dollar. Below the price scale, but still on the vertical axis, is another scale, which relates to the lines coming up from the bottom of the page and depicts volume. This scale represents numbers of shares traded and may be in 100s, 1,000s, or larger, depending upon how active a stock is being depicted.

Table 2–1 shows the data used to construct this chart. Each entry represents one day of trading, so the scale along the horizontal axis, being time, assigns one line for each day of trading. Longer-term charts could use each line to represent a week, a month, a quarter year, and so forth.

The important point to keep in mind is that the horizontal (X) axis is time. Placing a ruler along this axis, we can mark off equal time spans, regardless of the number of shares that change hands. A day in which a million shares change hands will occupy no more of the horizontal scale than a day in which 500 shares change hands. There is a small concession made to the market in that there is no gap left for weekends; a five-day trading week is assumed. Usually, however, a space is skipped for holidays, so a line is being assigned to a period when *nothing* happened.

Looking at the numbers in the table and relating them to the chart, we see that our first entry in the upper part of the chart is a heavy vertical line with its top at 38¾ and its bottom at 38. In other words, on that day the highest price was 38¾, the lowest price 38. There is also another small sideways line at the 38½ level, which indicates the price at which the stock closed on that day.

According to the table, 105,600 shares traded on that day. The volume is indicated by the line coming up from the bottom and ending just above the 1,000-volume level, since the scale is shown as volume in 100s.

Let us now take the same information in Table 2–1 and plot it in another manner. Instead of representing each day as a line, we will represent it as a rectangle. The highs will be similar to the highs on the bar chart, as will the lows, but the width of each rectangle will represent the volume traded during that day. In Figure 2–2, we have drawn such a chart. Each box follows its predecessor with no spaces left for weekends or holidays. We

Figure 2–1
BAR CHART

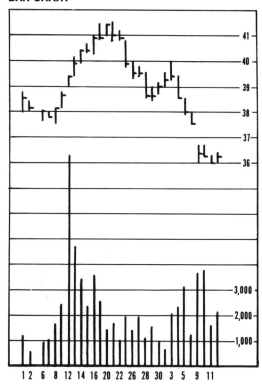

Table 2–1
BAR CHART DATA

Date		High	Low	Close	Volume in 100s
July	1	38¾	38	38½	1,056
	2	38⅜	38	38⅛	568
	6	38	37⅝	38	860
	7	38	37¾	37¾	963
	8	38⅛	37½	38⅛	1,596
	9	38¾	37⅛	38⅝	2,315
	12	39⅜	39	39⅜	8,182
	13	40⅛	39⅜	39⅞	4,660
	14	40⅜	39⅞	40⅜	3,396
	15	40⅝	40¼	40⅜	2,238
	16	41	40¼	40⅞	3,408
	19	41⅜	40¾	40⅞	2,475
	20	41⅜	41	41⅜	1,388
	21	41½	40¾	41	1,598
	22	41⅛	40¾	40⅞	975
	23	40¾	39¾	39⅞	1,883
	26	39⅞	39¼	39½	1,373
	27	39¾	39⅜	39½	1,728
	28	39½	38½	38⅝	1,025
	29	39	38⅜	38⅝	1,499
	30	39⅛	38⅝	39	909
August	2	39½	39	39¼	626
	3	40	39¼	39⅜	2,004
	4	39⅜	38½	38½	2,293
	5	38½	37⅞	38	3,148
	6	38	37½	37½	1,187
	9	36⅝	36	36⅜	3,587
	10	36⅝	36¼	36½	3,634
	11	36¼	36	36	1,551
	12	36⅜	36	36¼	2,087

Figure 2–2
EQUIVOLUME CHART

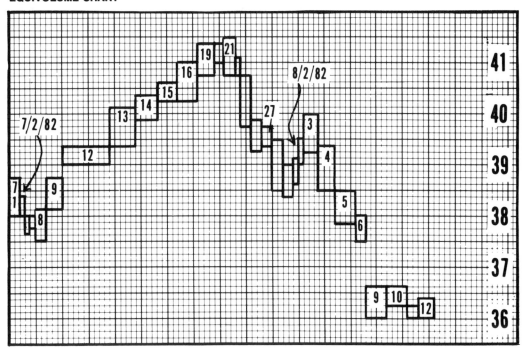

now have eliminated time from our horizontal (X) axis and substituted volume. This means that by laying a ruler horizontally along the chart we can measure distances of equal volume, rather than equal time—hence the name Equivolume Charting.

We have now a chart that is easier to read and easier to construct. Even though we have eliminated time as a dimension on the chart, we have not lost the ability to recognize each individual day. If we like, we can write the date in each box in order to be able to see when certain events took place.

It will be noticed that we dropped the closing price information from these charts. People who feel more comfortable retaining this information can make a mark in each box showing the closing price. We feel, however, that it is unnecessary. The closing price is only one trade during the day, and that happens to be the last one. We see no reason to place any special significance on this number.

The volume scale is the only part of this chart that has changed from the older method. Essentially, we have chosen a volume scale that will depict the stock in an understandable manner. We would like low-volume days such as the second, third, and fourth days to appear as very narrow days, whereas the heavier volume days should be emphasized by spreading laterally across the page into wide entries. The seventh entry, July 12, for example, represents a day of extremely heavy trading. Over 800,000 shares changed hands in the stock on that day, putting it near the top of the most active list. On the bar chart, it looks no different than any other day. On the Equivolume chart, it is nine times as wide as the very light volume days of a few days earlier.

A more precise way of arriving at a volume scale entails the averaging of volume for a reasonable time preceding the beginning of the chart and using two thirds of that average number as the scale. We found that in the 30 days of trading preceding the period on Table 2–1, the stock averaged almost 150,000 shares of trading per day. Two thirds of 150,000 being 100,000, we used 100,000 shares as our *volume increment*. This means that we plotted our chart by assigning one column on the chart to every 100,000 shares *or any part thereof.* If the stock traded under 100,000 shares, our entry would be one column wide on the chart. For example, on July 2, the volume was 56,800 shares. This is under 100,000 shares, so it is posted as only one space wide. At exactly 100,000, we would still be at one space wide; but if the volume crossed that line at all, even by only 100 shares, making it 100,100, we would go another *full* space to the right and make the entry two columns wide. Similarly, at 200,100 or more we would go to the third column, and so on. The July 9 entry is 231,500, which exceeds 200,000 and puts us into the third column, so the day is plotted three columns wide. On August 5 the volume was 314,800 shares, so it is depicted on the chart occupying four columns.

A less active stock might have far lower daily volume and, therefore, a lower volume increment, but the rules would be the same. If, for example, the volume increment were 5,000 shares, we would move sideways one column *for every 5,000 shares or any part thereof.* A day in which 4,700 shares traded would be one wide, a day of 5,000 shares would still be one wide, but a day of 5,100 would be two wide. The next crossover would be at 10,000, the next at 15,000, and so on.

Choosing the vertical (price) scale is a matter of convenience. In most charts we scale the price as in Figure 2–2, using one point per major division. However, a very volatile stock might tend to make the entries too tall to be easily interpreted, and a squeezed scale where we used one major division for every two points would be more in order. Such a scale is usually necessary in a high-priced stock also. Sometimes it is helpful to plot a very low-priced stock on an expanded scale wherein each major division represents only one-half point of trading. The vertical dimension of the boxes is thereby enlarged, and the entries become more significant. Ideally, we would like to have chart patterns look somewhat alike in different stocks, regardless of price level and volatility. We can get closer to this ideal by using an appropriate price scale.

Sometimes an inactive stock will change in character, both in terms of price movement and volume. At such a time it is worthwhile to go back and restructure our chart, using a new price scale and/or a new volume increment. Using the wrong scales can lead us to the making of bad decisions or the missing of good opportunities.

Should a stock split take place in a stock we are charting, it can usually be accommodated on the existing chart, by adjusting *both* scales. On a 2-for-1 split, for example, the price of the stock is halved, and the number of shares outstanding is doubled. Consequently, we would make our adjustments by renumbering our price scale to half the price and by doubling the volume increment. Since there is twice as much stock available for trading, we want it to take twice as many shares of volume to move our postings laterally a given amount.

We have now learned how to construct an Equivolume chart. In later chapters, we will be working with these charts in a number of ways. The importance of this method of charting stems from the nontime X-axis. We are now looking at the market in its own terms—volume, not time.

In this chapter, we have constructed a daily-based chart, where each entry represents one day of trading. This charting method can also be used effectively using longer time periods and relating them to the volume during those time periods. In later sections, we will work with weekly-based and even monthly-based charts. All of the construction methods remain the same as in the daily charts except that the volume intervals will, of course, be larger, since we are looking at a week or a month of trading at a time.

Chapter 3   Box Shapes and Their Meaning

Now that we have our little boxes properly marching across the paper, we need to know what these little boxes mean. We have said that each box is telling us a story; now we must learn how to interpret that story.

The first thing to keep in mind is that the shape of a box is as important as its size. Its shape is giving us an accurate indication of the supply and demand equilibrium for that stock on that day. If a stock doubles its volume and also doubles its price range from one day to another, there is no difference in the shape of the two boxes, but there is a great difference in their sizes. The shape and size are relaying two different pieces of information. The first—shape—tells us how easy or hard it is for that stock to move on that day. The second—the size—reflects overall interest in the action taking place.

Box shapes should always be compared to other boxes on the same chart, since the scales used can determine whether a stock produces mostly very square boxes or mostly tall thin boxes. From now on, we will refer to a box that is much taller than it is wide as a *narrow* day, a day in which width and height are about equal as a *square* day, and a day in which the box formed is much wider than it is high as an *oversquare* day. The relative shapes of boxes will be our main concern. If, due to our scales, most entries are quite square, a narrow day may not appear as dramatically as it would on a chart with a higher volume increment, but its relative narrowness would still be significant.

Narrow boxes indicate ease of movement; they show us that a stock is having little difficulty progressing in its chosen direction. If the stock were moving up on a narrow day, we would know that buying pressure was much heavier than selling pressure. Buyers were having to bid the stock up in order to find stock to buy. We would say the stock is moving up easily because it is not taking much buying to move the price.

Figure 3–1, a five-month period of trading in Polaroid in the spring and summer of 1982, shows us a great variety in box sizes and box shapes. Days marked 1 and 2 are narrow boxes, but on relatively light volume and within a sideways trading range. They are light volume attempts at a rally which is unable to gather a following. Prior to the period charted, the stock had been in a long decline, and these preliminary rally attempts were ineffectual. They were showing, however, that the stock could move upward quite easily. Day 3 is a much heavier volume day, but still a narrow day due to the wide spread. The stock is again probing higher levels and finding little resistance, but the buyers still do not have enough muscle, and the stock quickly drops back. The next significant narrow day is marked 4. The stock has been in a decline for some time, has gone to new lows, and is almost in free fall on this day. There is little resistance to the move as the stock falls below $17. The next narrow day, 5, is the reversal of day 4 and is only

Figure 3–1
POLAROID DAILY (interval: 50,000 shares)

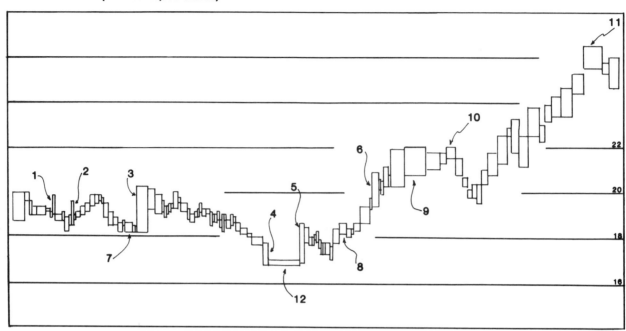

two days later. Suddenly the stock is finding it very easy to move upward. We see later, of course, that this was the first rally in an important change in direction for the stock. Another day of easy movement is seen at 6. By now, the stock has started on its advance and is moving up with ease. Buyers are continuing to pay up to acquire stock. The narrowness of the move, combined with its overall size, tells us that a strong move is underway.

Now, let us look at some square days. A square day indicates difficulty of movement. If a stock has been moving up and starts to develop squares, the buyers are meeting with heavier selling. They are able to buy without moving the price. It indicates an area where there is stock for sale and, if the sellers are strong enough, may be a point at which the stock will turn down. Conversely, square formations after a decline indicate that the sellers who have been forcing prices lower have encountered a level at which there is a heavier buying interest. Their selling is no longer dropping prices easily, since there is evidently a reservoir of buyers ready to accumulate their stock.

We see such a square at day 7. It is the same level at which prices turned higher a few weeks before. Evidently, the buyers are willing to accept all stock offered, so prices hold steady and a wide short day develops. It is this support, and a temporary triumph on the part of the buyers, which leads to the rally we saw on narrow day 3.

Square day 8 comes in as the stock tries to get through the highs of the prior rally. There are still sellers waiting there, and they stop the stock from advancing. Three days later, the same thing happens again before the stock finally breaks through the resistance and resumes its advance.

Day 9 is particularly significant. Not only is it square, but it is very large. Extremely heavy volume has developed, but the buyers have run into a barracade of sellers. A lighter volume rerun is seen three days later at 10, and this leads to a substantial pullback during the next week.

Day 11 has all of the characteristics of 9. The stock has found another level at which sellers are powerful enough to stop the heavy volume advance. It should serve as a warning that another pullback may be imminent.

Our chart contains only one really impressive oversquare day, but it is a classic example of demand overcoming supply. Day 12 consists of huge volume, after a downward move, in an extremely small trading range. The sellers who were in control at narrow day 4 have suddenly run into a stone wall. Volume expands dramatically as they try to push prices lower but see their shares accepted by a determined group of buyers. It is much like a compressed spring. On the next day, the sellers have run out of strength, the pressure is taken off the compressed spring, and prices bounce upward on day 5.

The shape of each box is telling us a story, and our careful attention to that story can help us greatly in anticipating future price moves. Our concern is ease of movement. We can ask each box to tell us how hard or easy it is to move in the direction it is trying to go. The short fat ones are having trouble running, while the tall thin ones are sprinting with little effort.

Box shape is not the only value to Equivolume Charting, but these building blocks are the foundation on which the rest is built. The first step in understanding a stock is to analyze this foundation, and then to move on to the more complex ways in which groups of boxes give us additional information.

Chapter 4   Consolidation Formations

When we start to put boxes together on a chart it becomes evident that there are three different phases in price movement: upward moves, downward moves, and sideways moves. In this chapter, we will study sideways moves of various sorts and try to see what information they can impart.

These lateral trading ranges can be large or small, narrow or wide, converging or parallel. Some are only pauses in a move, while others are a turning point. All of them, however, represent a price range wherein buyers and sellers are at a standoff. At least temporarily, neither group can maintain control. The buyers move the stock to the upper limits of the area but fail to keep the rally going. The sellers then take over and move prices back down to the lower limits of the area. Eventually one group or the other will succeed in moving the stock out of the consolidation area and a worthwhile price move will ensue.

The main point to remember is that consolidation areas are not times to buy a stock nor to short a stock. The stock is moving sideways, and may come out of it in either direction. Once it comes out of the consolidation, an opportunity does exist, since a direction has been indicated.

In the meantime, there is not usually room to make a reasonable profit within the limits of the trading range, and the risks are too high. The stock will eventually move out of the trading range, and will probably move quite rapidly. It may be in your favor, but then again it may move against you. In addition, there is no way to know how long the trading range is going to last, and during that time your money will not be working for you. An aggressive investor measures results against time. Lost time while a stock is in a consolidation phase is lost money, in that the money could have been producing capital gains in another stock which *was* moving.

This is not to say, however, that consolidation areas are useless. Price moves are usually proportional to their preceding consolidation areas. The more stock traded in a consolidation, the larger the move once the stock breaks out. It is a cause-and-effect relationship, and will be discussed further in Chapter 6.

The most typical consolidation area is rectangular. The lows and highs are confined within two price levels. Let us look at Figure 4–1, a daily chart of Technicolor during the spring and summer of 1981. The first part of the chart consists of a rectangular consolidation that lasted 20 days. The top of the area was at 24½, the low at 22. The stock bumped repeatedly against these levels without getting through them.

It should be noticed that volume tended to decrease as we moved across the area. This is typical of consolidations. Volume gets lighter as both buyers and sellers become exhausted trying to force the stock in their direction. We also see here that the easier movement seems to be on the upward moves.

Figure 4–1
TECHNICOLOR—DAILY (interval: 5,000 shares)

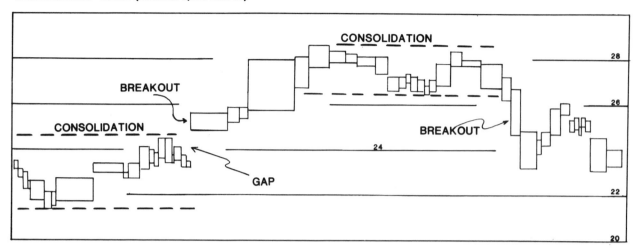

It is at least a clue that the eventual breakout will be to the upside. The breakout, when it finally happens, is dramatic. The buyers have taken control. Volume increases as the stock moves away from the consolidation area.

It is not long thereafter that another rectangular consolidation starts to form. The square and oversquare days indicate an end to the advance and a broad sideways move begins. As before, we see a decrease in volume across the area, and we can observe that the most square days are coming at the tops of rallies rather than at the bottom of declines. This is telling us the sellers are more likely to be triumphant than are the buyers. The move is, in fact, to the downside, and is unmistakable due to the narrow day on the breakout.

In Figure 4–2, we see another major consolidation, this time in Conoco in 1980. After a long decline the stock starts to move sideways between 41 and 45½. There is little here to tell us if it is only catching its breath prior to going lower, or reversing to an uptrend. Ease of movement seems similar in both directions. There is a sideways rectangular pattern, however, which indicates a buying or shorting opportunity is in the offing. The breakout above 45½ is made with a tall, thin day and indicates the probable future direction of the stock. After a somewhat terrifying pullback, the stock does go substantially higher.

Often, sideways moves tend to show a convergence of the highs and lows rather than a parallelism. As the consolidation progresses, the buyers and sellers get closer to one another. There still tends to be a decrease in volume across the area and then a dramatic move as the limits of the consolidation are violated. Figure 4–3 shows such a sideways move in Weyerhauser during early 1981. We have outlined the triangular consolidation, followed by the downside breakout. There is not only a decrease in volume across the area but a decrease in spreads as well. Finally, at the apex of the triangle, the drop begins. There were no volume clues in this formation to indicate the direction of the eventual move.

In all of these examples, we have seen that the move out of the consolidation area was quite spectacular. Volume and range increased as the stock burst out of the levels which were restricting it. A move out of a consolidation area should be one of unusual proportions. Any other kind should be suspect. A light-volume dip below the support level may have little meaning, since the sellers could not gather a following. Even heavy volume, if not accompanied by a substantial move, loses its credibility. The sellers have tried very

Figure 4–2
CONOCO—DAILY (interval: 50,000 shares)

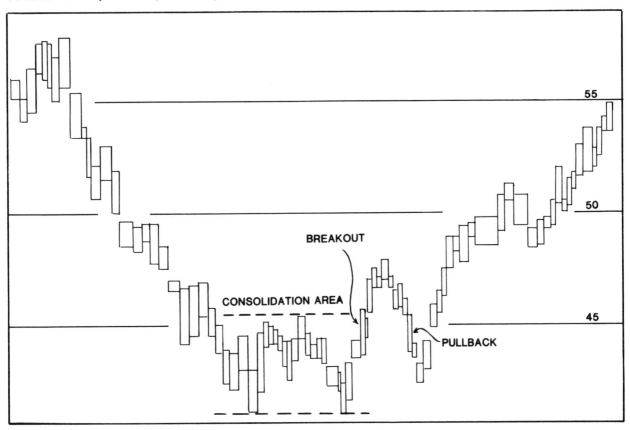

Figure 4–3
WEYERHAUSER—DAILY (interval: 40,000 shares)

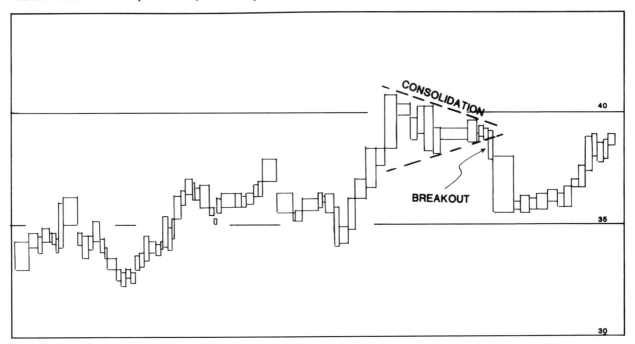

hard to force prices lower but have met with concentrated buying just below the old support area. Similarly, moves to the upside should, to be believable, have increasing volume and a widening of the spread.

An encouraging sign accompanying a breakout is the development of a gap, that is, an area between the two boxes where no trading took place. Such a gap is shown in Figure 4–1. This is usually termed a breakaway gap, since the stock is breaking away from a consolidation area.

As can be seen, consolidations in themselves are not investment opportunities, but they are the breeding ground for profits. A stock which moves spectacularly out of a large consolidation area has announced its intentions loudly, and presents a very good opportunity. Buying on breakouts means never buying a stock on its low. The stock has to have formed a sideways area and then started to move. It also means that the investor is less likely to be in an inactive situation. He moves into a stock because it has started to act well, not because it looks cheap. Buying stocks because they "can't go any lower" is likely to be extremely costly. We want to own stocks that are doing well, not stocks that are on lows.

Similarly, stocks should never be shorted because they look too high, only because they are acting poorly. A break to the downside out of a consolidation can be a very good signal to go short.

Does the above discussion imply that we should not take profits because a stock looks too high or cover shorts because a stock looks too low? No! We have learned that box shapes often indicate the termination of a move, and those signals may be used to take profits. After a move terminates, it is likely that the stock will move sideways in a consolidation area. There is no point in holding through the area, not knowing whether the move will resume or a reversal will take place. During the consolidation, the money is inactive and could probably be used better in another situation. We can always come back to this stock when it again breaks out in either direction.

The next few chapters will have more to say about the recognition of tops and bottoms. These are areas for taking profits, *not* areas for initiating new positions. Stocks have three phases: up, sideways, and down. We want to be out of the stocks during the sideways moves, but we must be watching them for an opportunity.

Chapter 5   Stocks on the Move

In the last chapter, we saw that we want only to buy stocks that are moving up, and only to short stocks that are moving down. Breakouts from consolidations are the best time to initiate these positions. Once a stock is moving, however, we need to know the difference between a pause in the move and an end to the move. We don't want to take a 3-point profit if the stock is going to move 10 or 20 points. Equivolume charts can be very helpful in this regard.

We know that narrow days indicate ease of movement and wide days indicate difficulty of movement. Throughout a move we must constantly ask ourselves if the stock is still moving easily. No move is without its occasional pullbacks, and those pullbacks must not be mistaken for a termination of the move. The clues are box shape and box size. A major move will usually end with one or more square or oversquare boxes, as supply battles with demand. A temporary resting point is more likely to start with a narrow day in the direction of movement, followed by lighter volume and more square days in the opposite direction.

Figure 5–1 shows Atlantic Richfield in mid-1980. After the sideways move that occupies much of the chart, the breakout to the upside is very spectacular, in that volume and range both increase. There is also a gap, showing the power of the breakout. After two more days of strength, the stock starts back down. Here we see that the pullback is on lighter trading and the days are somewhat more square than on the prior upmove. In addition, the topping day was not at all square. It appears that the move has further to go. The last day on the chart penetrates the prior high with increasing volume but with sufficient spread, confirming the upward direction of the stock.

Figure 5–2 shows a number of pullbacks in Heublein after a classic breakout. In the first drop, volume is light and follows an insignificant top. The stock then forms a fairly wide area of reconsolidation before the next upleg. The second top has more squareness to it, but the pullback again is on lighter trading and is unable to get anywhere. The third top is quite different, however. It is a much heavier volume day and is quite square. The subsequent retreat shows easier movement to the downside and would indicate a probable decline, or at least another broad sideways area as a prognosis.

There was a gap on the original breakout, and another breakaway gap on the start to the second top. Both show power in the stock, since the day after the gap does not indicate great difficulty of movement. There is also a gap as the third leg starts, which looks healthy, but the final gap on the upmove must cause us additional worry. The day after the gap is quite square, and comes after a long upward move. Often a stock will gap as the

Figure 5–1
ATLANTIC RICHFIELD (interval: 80,000 shares)

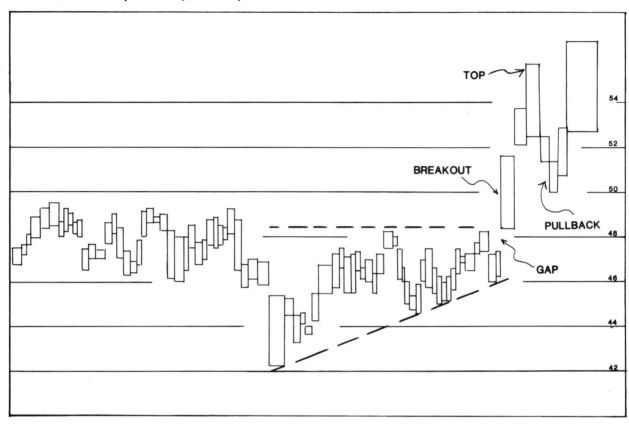

last upthrust is completed. The heavier volume and the square day indicate that this is an *exhaustion gap,* and a bad sign not a good sign.

The shape of the boxes on the two sides of any gap indicate their significance. A gap occurring between a square box and a narrow box generally is a *breakaway gap,* whereas a gap going from a narrow box to a square box usually indicates exhaustion. Narrow boxes on both sides of the gap

Figure 5–2
HEUBLEIN—DAILY (interval: 10,000 shares)

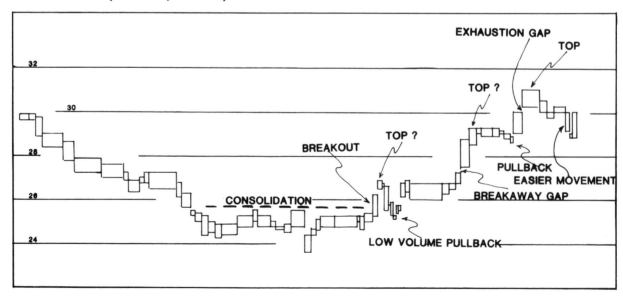

indicate that a powerful move is underway. They usually occur during an extended move and are a sign that it has further to go. We call these *continuation gaps*. If the boxes on both sides of a gap are square or small, they usually mean very little. Such gaps are often seen within consolidation formations.

Once a stock appears to have terminated its move, profits should be taken. Sometimes what appeared to be the end of the move is seen in retrospect to have been only a larger pullback. However, positions can be reestablished after the sideways move if this is the case.

We will see, in the chapter on trend lines and curvilinear channels, that there are other clues besides box shape and box size to indicate the end of a move. Pullbacks tend to stay within the trend, while major turning points violate the trend. In addition, the next chapter on symmetry and objectives helps to recognize the probable extent of a move. If we can project approximately when we expect a move to end, we can discount a questionable-looking pullback which occurs before we reach the objective.

Chapter 6　　　Symmetry and Objectives

Wouldn't it be nice if we knew how far a stock move would carry? If we could predict when the next top was going to occur, we would have less trouble differentiating between pullbacks and tops. Our trend lines help somewhat in this regard, as does a study of box shapes and box sizes. It is still easy, however, to get out too soon and miss a large part of a move. It is also easy to stay too long and lose a large part of our profits by not recognizing a top when it occurs.

There *is* a way of judging the probable extent of a move. It is not exact, and should not be relied upon when other signals tell us that a move is over, but it is a valuable confirmation if we are in doubt. It relies upon the fact that there is a direct cause-and-effect relationship in the market, and that the cause and effect are volume-related.

Whenever a stock is in a consolidation area, stock is changing hands without a significant price move. As we have said earlier, a battle is going on between buyers and sellers. New buyers are accumulating stock in anticipation of an upward move. The eventual move out of the congestion area will determine whether or not they were correct. If the breakout is to the upside, we have a large group of new holders who will be anxious to take profits as the move progresses. If, on the other hand, the move is to the downside, the same people—those who bought in the consolidation area—will be selling as their fear level increases. In either case, we have a reservoir of sellers who accumulated a certain number of shares during the consolidation. It is this group of new holders that determines the probable extent of the ensuing move. They are the cause which brings about the eventual effect. The more stock they bought in the consolidation, the more stock they will have to distribute after the move starts. Unless there has been a substantial change in the stock, bringing in new buyers or sellers from the sidelines, we can therefore expect a direct relationship between the number of shares traded in a consolidation area and the number of shares traded in the subsequent move.

It should be noted that we are talking about shares in the move, not points of movement. The vertical extent of the move is a function of the slope. A steep advance will carry the stock to much higher prices while the predetermined number of shares change hands; a slow advance may only develop small profits. The relationship is one of volume to volume, which means horizontal distances on an Equivolume chart.

In order to establish an objective for a move, we must wait until after a breakout has occurred and then measure, horizontally on our chart, the width of the consolidation. By marking off the same distance again, we would have some idea when the stock will run out of volume and be ready for a reversal.

In Figure 6–1 we have followed this procedure on a weekly-based chart of International Paper. Distance A–B is the volume of trading during the consolidation. The breakout at B tells us that the consolidation is over and the stock is moving higher. Distance B–C is our projected volume to the top. We would expect the stock to move higher until we reached point C in our volume measurement. The stock does, in fact, stop moving up in that area and forms a small consolidation top. The width of that top, in turn, is quite narrow, indicating that the next move is not likely to last long in terms of volume. The D–E distance implies a low in the area we have marked F. The stock then goes through a new consolidation between G and H, which is quite wide. We know as we approach H that the eventual move could be large enough to be profitable, be it up or down. The breakout at H says the move is up, and as we go off the margin of the chart we can project approximately where we expect the move to end.

There are two reasons for making objective projections. The first is in order to know when a move is likely to terminate. The second is its use in the selection of stocks to trade. A wide base is more likely to generate a substantial move than is a narrow base. Sharp bottoms on little volume do not have the cause to create a large effect.

An investor should be aware of the width of consolidation areas and act on stocks which have dramatic moves out of fairly long sideways areas.

Figure 6–2 is another example of objective projection. After a long decline in Union Oil of California, a good base is built. At the point of breakout we can measure A–B and therefore project point C. As can be seen, the stock attains point C and then gets very square. The move appears to be over at this point, and the stock should be sold.

Another helpful tool, closely allied to objective determination, is a part of the next major section of this book, dealing with cycles. It is the symmetry of the patterns. The use of symmetry is merely the realization that most up and down moves tend to be quite regular. The volume in the down move usually is quite similar to the volume in the upmove, so that the waves look smooth and regular. By anticipating symmetry, we can often know when a move is not yet completed. Not enough trading has taken place to

Figure 6–1
INTERNATIONAL PAPER—WEEKLY (interval:100,000 shares)

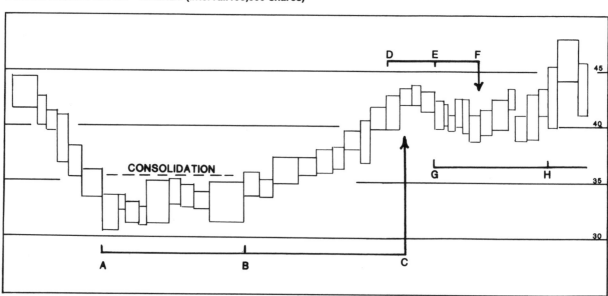

Figure 6–2
UNION OIL OF CALIFORNIA—WEEKLY (interval:100,000 shares)

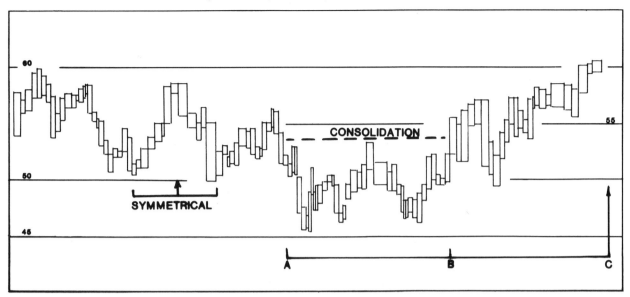

make the pattern symmetrical. Symmetrical moves are most apparent in stocks moving sideways on a longer-term basis. As will be discussed in the cycle sections, the symmetry can be affected by the longer-term direction of a move. Figure 6–2 shows a typical symmetrical cycle.

Chapter 7   Curvilinear Channels

Since the first publishing of *Profits in Volume,* it has been necessary to make very few changes in the utilization of Equivolume charts. At this point, we do make one major change, however. In following the methodology of other forms of technical analysis, we found it logical to utilize their procedures. This included trend lines. A trend line is a *straight* line drawn on a chart that helps to define the price trend of that stock. It is constructed from top to top of each rally during a decline, and from bottom to bottom of each pullback during an advance, in order to recognize the slope of the move. It is assumed that a penetration of the trend line indicates a change of direction.

We hereby abandon straight lines and substitute curved lines in their place. We have found that earlier signals are developed in this way, helping to retain a larger part of our profits.

Stocks live in a world of their own—a natural world, not a human world. We expect them to follow straight lines because we like straight lines. This is wrong. The price and volume of a stock are based upon changing conditions, and these changes are usually gradual. Supply overcomes demand over a period of time, and that change follows a curve. It is not a straight line.

Straight lines are a concept of man. Nature does not operate in straight lines. A pool of water, with no forces of wind or current on it, does have a flat surface; but let any breeze play across its surface and the pattern is broken—ripples and waves develop. A stock is not a stagnant, breezeless pool. It is dynamic. It has forces acting upon it and these forces are causing changes, changes which are reflected in gradual movement.

Nowhere in nature do we see dynamic systems that produce straight lines. Newtonian physics tells us that an object traveling in a straight line will continue to travel in a straight line unless acted upon by an exterior force. A stock is always being pushed and pulled by innumerable exterior forces. Every time a share is bought or sold, that action causes a reaction on the part of the stock's supply-demand equilibrium. Newton also told us that every action has an equal and opposite reaction. These are the forces that overcome the inertia of straight-line movement.

In the highland of Peru, there is an area crisscrossed by straight lines. They have been postulated to be landing strips of aircraft or spacecraft. Their significance lies in the fact that they are straight. Their very straightness is the tipoff that they are not natural, but man-made. Some intelligent being must have had a part in their construction, or they would not be straight.

The moon rotates around the sun; the earth and planets follow eliptical orbits, as do the comets. Every 250 million years, the sun orbits around the center of the galaxy. All are dynamic systems, acted upon by exterior forces, and none follow straight lines. True, the galaxies appear to be diverging in straight lines from the center of the big bang nucleus; but even in this case, Einsteinian theory tells us that they are following the path of a curving universe.

Back to stocks and straight edges. If we can, as we must, consider a stock as a dynamic system, then we must also expect it to act as a dynamic system would. Consequently, we must put away the straight edges and start drawing curved lines, lines that reflect the gradual changes being brought about by external forces.

The traditional method of drawing trend lines is shown in Figure 7–1. Here we see Inexco during mid-1981. The stock went through a major advance, followed by a similar decline. Reviewing what we learned in previous chapters, we conclude that the stock is in a consolidation during the first part of the chart—a believable analysis, since the breakout is to the upside on much heavier volume. Its squareness, however, leads to a quick pullback, but on low volume, producing little concern. Also, the top which leads to the pullback is in no way alarming. The next upmove confirms the strength due to its narrowness. A second pullback is similar—still not time to sell. A few days later, however, the days become more square and progress to the upside is very difficult. It appears that a top may be forming.

A confirmation that the move is over can be derived by using trend lines. Line A–B was the first trend line drawn, and was based upon the slope of the first two bottoms. Later, as it becomes obvious that the stock is in a more rapid advance, a second trend line (C–D) can be drawn. These trend lines are defined by connecting two or more pullbacks during an advance; and similarly, in a decline, by connecting two or more rallies.

Based upon the more conservative A–B trend line, an owner would not sell his stock until the trend line was penetrated at Sell #1. Based upon the less conservative trend line C–D, he would sell at Sell #2.

Stocks in an advance tend to accelerate the move, curving the pattern upward as they near the top. In the same way, stocks in a decline tend to

Figure 7–1
INEXCO—DAILY (interval:20,000 shares)

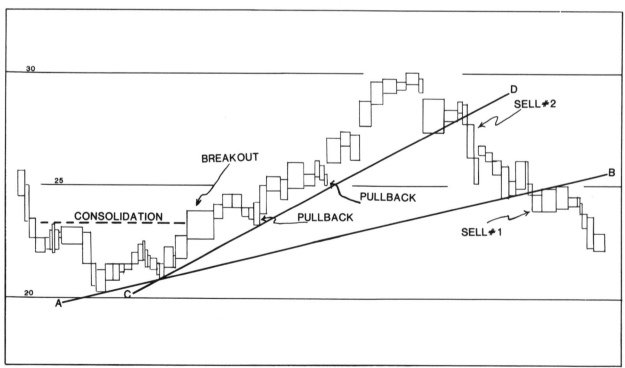

Figure 7–2
INEXCO—DAILY (interval: 20,000 shares)

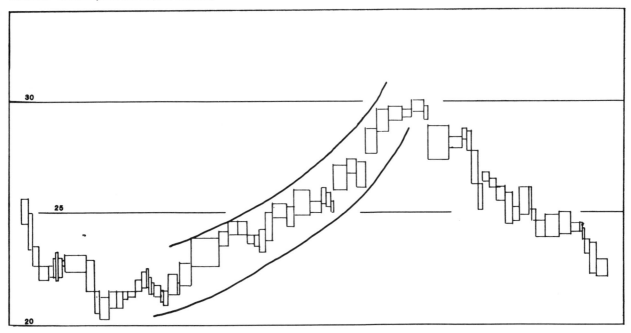

drop quickly in the last phases of the downmove. A straight line cannot follow this curved pattern without giving late signals. We suggest using a curved pair of lines that follow the pattern.

In Figure 7–2 we have drawn in such curved trend lines on the same chart as Figure 7–1. The procedure consists of drawing a line along the *tops* rather than the bottoms, and then drawing another line parallel to it along the bottoms. The position of the bottom line is dependent upon the upper line, which was drawn first. As can be seen, we are now defining the move much more closely than we could have with a straight line. Usually the bottom line will not be penetrated during pullbacks, but will be penetrated when a real decline begins. Using this method, we not only get out at a

Figure 7–3
BURLINGTON INDUSTRIES—WEEKLY (interval: 100,000 shares)

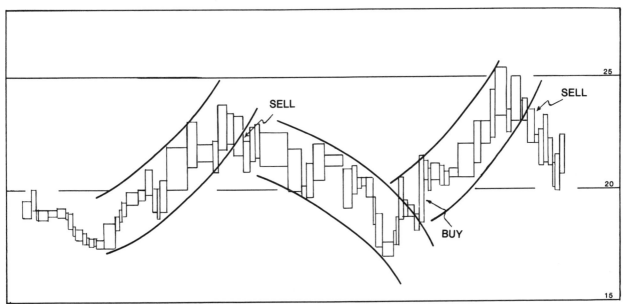

better price, but we get out sooner, allowing us to move on to another opportunity.

Figure 7–3 is a weekly chart rather than a daily chart, so we are looking at longer time spans and more substantial moves. The results are similar, however. We see three distinct moves, all of which could have been very profitable. In each section of the chart, we have drawn in curvilinear channels which would have been easy to identify while the moves were in progress, and which would have gotten us out with a profit in each case. The first channel was almost straight, and a ruler-drawn trend line would probably have done as well. The second curves sharply downward toward the end of the move, so our curved lines would have helped to lock in more of the profit. In the third case, the move accelerated on the upside, curving our channel upward. A straight line would have gotten us out at a lower price, and it would have been weeks later.

Channels are a very valuable tool in recognizing the termination of a move, but should not be relied on solely. Box shape and size are additional clues, as seen in Chapter 5. Similarly, symmetry and objectives, the subject of the last chapter, can provide additional information. All of these methods should be consulted in making a decision.

Part Two   Volume Cycles

Chapter 8   The Logic of Volume Cyclicality

As Stone Age men stood on a cliff overlooking the endless expanses of the Indian Ocean and saw the waves rolling in toward the shore of Africa, they must have been struck by the rhythmic regularity. The huge rollers marched toward shore in a steady cadence from as far away as the eye could see. They noticed that on some days the waves were higher than on other days, that at times they were closer together or further apart, but that on any given observation there was a regularity, a rhythm. The rollers crashed on the rocks and sluiced back through the crevices with a monotonous precision, like the beating of a drum.

Later, the Polynesian navigators, the most important passengers on the great war canoes, were able to guide their people across vast expanses of the Pacific Ocean in an almost magical manner. Their secret was a stick chart—a map which told them what the wave patterns looked like in different parts of the ocean. They knew that the direction and formation of the waves changed as the great Pacific swells were deflected by the islands they encountered, and the patterns were altered. The woven sticks of their chart depicted those waves, their direction, their interaction, their cross currents.

Primitive people throughout the world observed the regularity of the skies above them. The moon went through regular cycles from new moon to full moon and back. The stars followed seasonal patterns, which told them when to plant their crops and when to harvest them. The planets, in their own rhythm, followed patterns independent of the stars. The Chinese and the Aztecs both developed extremely accurate calendars based upon the motion of the heavens. The rhythm of the skies became a predictive tool, allowing them to look into the future, knowing what the heavens would look like months later. The predictability of regularly recurring events was their crystal ball. They lived by the cycles and rhythm of the universe.

Here we must distinguish between cyclicality and rhythm. We tend to talk about cycles when we may really mean rhythms. The word *cycle* has its origins in the Greek word *kyklos,* which simply means a circle. The interesting thing about a circle is that as we go around it we eventually come back where we started. A cycle therefore eventually brings us back to our point of origin. A cycle, then, is a return to a starting point. There is no requirement for regularity, but only a return.

Rhythm, on the other hand, carries the additional requirement of regularity. We normally look for a regularity in terms of time, expecting a return to the point of origin on a regular time interval.

The word rhythm has its basis in the Latin word *rhythmus*, which traces back to the Greek's *rhythmos* and *rhein*, meaning to flow. This is also the basis of our word *stream*. The rhythm we are concerned with is closely related to the flow of a stream. These are the cycles which also have to meet the requirement of repeating on a regular basis, usually on a time-measured regularity.

Can we doubt the regularity of nature? Halley's Comet sling-shots around the sun in a spectacular display every 75 years. The sun circles the center of the galaxy every 250 million years. Pulsars send their message over millions of light years that there is a regularity, a rhythm. Closer to home, the tides ebb and flow in their twice daily pattern, and lemmings march to the sea every four years. The pattern of the seasons is a predictive tool which prompts us to buy a winter coat in September and order flower seeds in midwinter.

Man is a part of nature; the rhythms of the universe are the rhythms of mankind. Our hearts beat within us in a regular manner, sustaining us with their rhythmic beats. When the rhythm stops, so does life. As the pace of living becomes more stressful, the tempo increases; as we sleep, the pace slows. It is a rhythm, but a variable rhythm based upon changing conditions. Like the various movements of a Beethoven sonata there are the largos and the adagios, but the cyclicality remains throughout the music, and the rhythm of each movement remains the same.

If nature is rhythmic and the heavens are rhythmic, if the seas are rhythmic, and man himself is rhythmic, then should we not expect the pursuits of man to be rhythmic also? As lemmings troop to their death in a regular pattern, isn't it likely that investors will likewise tumble off the cliffs of bear markets? As day follows night and spring follows winter, shouldn't prosperity follow recession, and bull markets follow bear markets?

Certainly business is cyclical. There is always a return to the starting point; good times do follow bad. But cyclicality is not in itself sufficient as a predictive tool. It assures us that the cycle will eventually bring us back to the starting point, but it does not tell us when. We must ascertain more than cyclicality; we must find the rhythm.

The cyclicality of mankind may assure us that human ingenuity will lead us to times of new quests for knowledge eventually, but the Dark Ages lasted for hundreds of years before the age of Pericles was returned with the Renaissance.

Perhaps boom does follow bust and prosperity does come after a depression, but we must know *when* this is going to occur. One of the greatest traps in history was the market rally of 1930. The October 1929 crash destroyed the fortunes of many amateurs. The disaster of 1930–32 wiped out the sophisticates who had second-guessed the market top in October of 1929. They rushed to buy when they believed the bottom had been made in November of that same year. The market bottom was finally made in July of 1932.

Cyclicality and rhythm are not new ideas among market analysts. A later chapter will look at R. N. Elliot's work on cyclicality. The Elliot wave has been one of the most outstanding contributions to technical analysis. This work deals only with cyclicality, however, not rhythm. It identifies and catalogs repetitive patterns in the stock market, but does not attempt to answer the question of *when*.

Edward R. Dewey's fascinating investigations into cycles ranged from sun spots to grasshopper abundance, from rainfall to fish migration. He recognized a regular oscillation between periods of war and periods of peace, between periods of high incidence of heart disease and periods of low incidence of heart disease.

Dewey related his work also to financial fields and showed a regularity in the recurring cycles of such diverse fields as wheat and corn production, building construction, railway traffic, and insurance sales. When it came to Wall Street, he, by his own admission, found the cyclicality to be extremely complicated. It appeared that there were repetitive cycles, and even rhythms, but they were very difficult to isolate and even harder to use as a money-making tool. He did not try to relate cyclicality and rhythm to individual stocks, but only to the overall market.

Another most intriguing piece of work on cyclicality was done in 1926 by a Russian, N. D. Kondratieff. He observed a repetitive economic pattern which appeared to crest every half century or so.

Every investigator of market cycles, and there have been many, has been stopped by a single question: Why? Even if mathematics can show a repetitive pattern such as market peaks every 9.2 years or every 41 months, the same problem crops up. It would seem there should be a logical explanation for these patterns, yet none is forthcoming.

Perhaps we can clarify the complexity of stock market cycles and at the same time develop an answer to why if we begin to look at stocks in a new way—a volume way. Suppose that we have been using the wrong yardstick for measuring the market. Is there any reason why we should require the stock market to follow a time-based rhythm?

Man created the stock market and believed since he had created it, that it should act as a person would act. We measure lives in months, weeks, days, hours, and minutes. Our frame of reference is a time frame. We look about us and find that most recurring events do so every so often, as measured on our calendar or wristwatch. The stock market is not a person or a group of people. It is a dynamic system, changing rapidly, but only changing when the market is open and when stocks are being traded. If the market is closed, the system is unable to adjust for such pressures as world events bring to bear. Only when the market reopens does the adjustment take place. And the adjustment takes place by the trading of stocks.

We may look at innumerable fundamental factors that effect the value of stocks, but it is the trading, not fundamental factors, that actually moves the price of stocks. The fundamental factors first have to go through the process of dissemination to the public. This in turn affects the fear and greed levels of the myriad of owners or potential owners of the stocks. Their emotional responses to these factors cause them to buy or not to buy, to sell or not to sell, to liquidate gradually, or to dump their stock at any price. The trading determines the prices. At the heart of the market is trading. It is the dynamic force bringing about the final output, which is the price.

If the market were to be closed for a week or two, no trading would occur, and therefore prices would not be able to adjust for changes in the attitudes of the public. A cyclicality based on time would certainly not be operative during the interval. The Greek word *rhein,* which relates rhythm to a stream, assumes a steady flow. The market is not a steady flow in terms of time. It is only open six hours per day, and only then is it flowing; the rest of the day and on weekends and holidays the streambed is dry.

We contend that time is the wrong measurement for the stock market. Only when there is trading is anything happening, and the heavier the trading the more there is happening. Therefore, only through volume can we represent the steady flow of prices, the response to shifts in investor sentiment.

If we want to recognize rhythm in the market, we are going to have to realize that the market marches to a different drummer. That drumbeat is best recognized through Equivolume charts, since these charts measure the market by its volume. If there is a rhythm to stocks and markets, and if that rhythm is volume-related, then it should be most easily observed by using a graphic method keyed to volume.

Chapter 9   Finding the Waves

SCALING UP

The process of locating the waves on an Equivolume chart of a stock, or a market average, is based upon scaling upward from the smallest wave pattern to the largest wave pattern. Each wave, when defined, provides the information necessary to define the next larger wave. It is a mistake to try to scale downward. This is a haphazard approach that may cause the missing of a significant part of the cyclicality. There is a tendency, when one looks at a chart, to mentally pick out the largest waves first. Our experience has been that trying to work first with the larger wave can lead to mistakes—costly mistakes! Scaling *up* provides a discipline and makes the approach mechanical. By scaling up and following the method which we will demonstrate in this chapter, two analysts abiding by the same rules should arrive at nearly identical charts.

FINDING THE SMALLEST WAVE PATTERN

The smallest discernible pattern on any chart is the ripple pattern. It tends to be more erratic than the larger cyclical patterns, because it is reflecting every minor influence upon the stock, both external and internal. Here the overall market gyrations can have a noticeable effect upon the individual issue, and news items that momentarily affect an industry can cause minor moves. In the components in daily trading, every individual transaction can reflect its influence. An institution with a large block to sell can have a decided effect, an effect that will later become less significant as we move on to the larger patterns. Consequently, we do not expect any great parallelism nor any precise pattern when we outline the minor moves.

The first step is simple. Using straight lines, we connect the bottom right corners of ascending boxes and the bottom left corners of descending boxes with a dotted line as in Figure 9–1. Then we connect the top left corners of ascending boxes and the top right corners of descending boxes in the same way. In addition, in order not to have gaps in the line, we continue the dots along the sides of boxes where a change of direction from ascending to descending or from descending to ascending is taking place.

At the interior angle of changes of direction, the two lines will cross. The segments of these lines inside the crossover can be ignored or erased. Once the analyst gets used to doing the minor wave enclosure, he will just draw the outer lines, realizing the interior segments mean nothing.

One would expect to arrive at a jagged, sawtoothed pattern through this method, but in reality the straight lines tend to coalesce into a rather smooth pattern. The reason for this is, of course, the fact that the charts are volume-related. Heavier volume on tops and bottoms broadens the postings and tends to round turning areas.

Figure 9–1
CONSTRUCTION OF THE MINOR WAVE

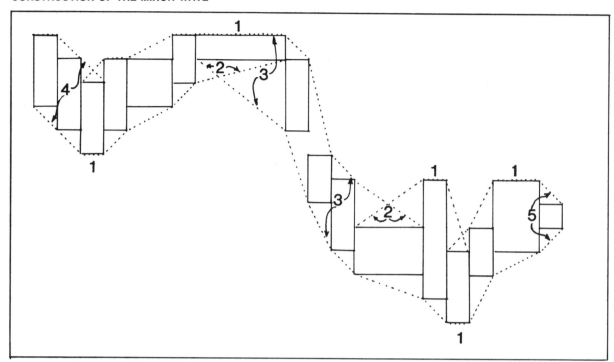

Figure 9–1 illustrates the enclosing of the minor wave. We have numbered significant areas referred to above.

At points 1, we have continued the line along the exterior of a turning point box.

At points 2, we indicate interior lines that can be eliminated. These are the interior angles of turning points.

This first pattern we have now defined does not necessarily consist of parallel lines. They can diverge from one another as at areas 3; they can be quite parallel as at area 4; or the can converge as at area 5.

We have defined a curvilinear pattern, with the many trading days merged into a stream of trading—a volume-based stream of trading. We are seeing the variation in supply and demand for the stock, as depicted by the Equivolume boxes, but they have now gained continuity and become a running pattern across the page.

The stream analogy can, in fact, be carried further and can help us to better visualize the forces that are acting on a stock. A declining stock can be thought of as a river. As the water rushes downhill and cuts its streambed, it tends to accelerate on the steeper slopes, cutting a straight and narrow channel. The volume of water is moving faster and therefore needs a narrower channel to carry the same amount of water. Consequently, the banks are close together and the channel has few twists or turns. Two forces are acting on the plunging water: One is gravity; the other is friction. On a steep slope the gravitational force is much more powerful than the friction as the water rushes over the bottom and sides of the channel. Sometimes there are boulders, large enough to turn the water aside temporarily, but their effect is only fleeting. Sometimes a very resistant shelf of rock will slow the water, only to produce a waterfall once the river gets past the obstruction. Above where the shelf occurs, the river will widen out into a pool, but below the waterfall the narrow channel will continue, as long as the slope is still steep.

So too with a stock as it is influenced by its two forces, supply and demand. A declining stock is being pushed downward by the gravity of supply, and being held back by the friction of demand. The supply is predominant, however, and, consequently, the slope is downward on our charts. With many heavy sellers and a few hesitant buyers the stock cuts a steep narrow channel. Pockets of heavier buying, like the boulders in our river, can only slightly deflect the plunge. Even larger buyers, like our shelves of resistant rock, only cause a pool, a sideways area; but once the buying is out of the way, we often encounter a waterfall. As we study cycles, we will see that some pauses are so transitory as to be almost indiscernible, since the primary force, gravity, is so powerful.

There comes a time, however, when our river comes out of the mountains and reaches the plains. The terrain levels out and the two forces, gravity and friction, are more in equilibrium. Now, instead of a straight, narrow channel, we have a much more twisting pattern. It takes less powerful forces to turn the water aside, so it meanders over the landscape. Usually, it follows a rather rhythmic course of twists and turns as the two nearly equal forces vie for control of the flow. Isn't this much like a stock in a sideways move? We get rhythmic patterns as first the buyers and then the sellers establish temporary control. Neither can maintain longer-term control, so the stock moves slowly back and forth. The streambed becomes wider also. The slower water flow necessitates more area to hold the water.

On our Equivolume chart, we are seeing more than just price change and direction; we are also seeing volume. A stock under heavy selling pressure will move downward in a narrow channel, with only moderate volume. At the sideways areas, we see congestion, the widening of the channel, as supply and demand are in equilibrium; consequently, volume will tend to increase.

In order to finish our analogy and look at rising stocks, we are going to have to postulate antigravity. Then our stream can run uphill as well as downhill. The restraining force is still friction, but now the friction in our stock is caused by supply while the antigravity force is demand. In all other ways, the action is the same. We have upside waterfalls, pools, cataracts, boulders. We are still dealing with forces, where one force is considerably stronger than the other.

Figure 9–2 is a daily-based Equivolume chart of Aetna. It represents a period of about 6½ months, from early March of 1981 to mid-September of the same year. Following the previously explained method, we have used a dotted line to connect the boxes and define the stream of trading. Henceforth, we will always use dotted lines for the minor wave pattern, dashed lines for the intermediate wave pattern, and solid lines for the major wave pattern. The analyst doing his own work, based on these methods, may find it more convenient to use solid lines made with colored felt-tip pens for every wave pattern, always assigning the same color to the same wave magnitude regardless of what chart is being analyzed.

In this chart, it should be noticed that the lines are not parallel. There are wider areas and narrower areas just as in our stream analogy. Areas marked 1 indicate ease of movement. The stock is in a narrow channel, finding little to hinder the progress. The dotted lines are very close to being parallel. We see this to a lesser extent at area 2. Although the lines are parallel, they are further apart because volume has been heavier. This is due to the fact that the stock was at this point in the final stages of an upmove. It was taking more buying pressure to overcome the selling pressure. At the two points marked 3, we see a waterfall and an antigravity waterfall.

It can be seen that the wave patterns are much more pronounced toward the left and right margins of the chart, where the stock was close to equilibrium. In both sections, the buyers and sellers were battling for control, so

Figure 9–2
AETNA—DAILY (interval: 50,000 shares; minor wave outlined)

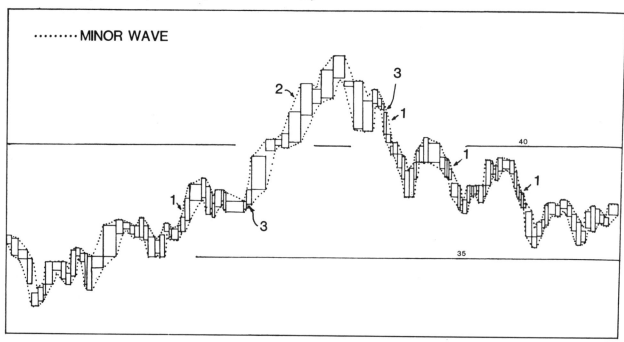

the stock meandered considerably. In the central section of the chart, during both the dramatic rise and the subsequent decline, there were strong forces at work. There was a large imbalance in these forces, so the waves become only hesitations, boulders in the stream.

It should also be apparent that there is, throughout the chart, a very rhythmic cyclicality. The tops and bottoms appear to be quite regular, giving the impression that there is a repetitive pattern. In the next chapter, we will delve into the recognition and interpretation of these patterns, but first we must have rules for recognizing these patterns.

THE INTERMEDIATE WAVE

Recognizing and identifying the important waves in one wave pattern always necessitates first finding the *next larger wave*. To see the waves correctly in the minor wave pattern, we must first draw in the next larger wave, the *intermediate wave pattern*. To do this, we will connect all of the prominent turning points in the minor wave pattern, much as we connected the boxes in constructing the minor wave. Now, however, we expect more parallelism, since the longer-term forces are becoming more apparent. Consequently, we will draw the curving lines in such a way that the upper and lower lines will never go in opposite directions from one another. If the top line is forced by the price action to go upward, then the bottom line must do the same. If a drop in price forces the lower line downward, the top line must follow, or approximately follow it. This means that the intermediate channel lines will not always intercept every turning point of the minor wave pattern.

In our example (Figure 9–3), this can be seen. We have enclosed the minor wave in the *smallest* comfortable channel. The width of the channel was dictated by the width of the most abrupt reaction moves we could see on the chart. In the area marked 1, the width of the upward channel was being defined by the extent of these pullbacks. The pullbacks were the maximum significant move apparent at that time, dictating the width of the channel within which the stock was moving and could be expected to move. As we

Figure 9–3
AETNA—DAILY (interval: 50,000 shares; minor and intermediate waves outlined)

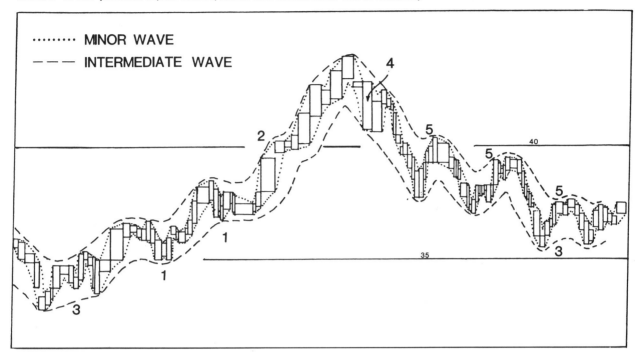

entered into the fast rising phase of the stock action at area 2, the channel might have been drawn narrower, since the pullbacks were, in that area, very minor; but we maintained the width, waiting for further evidence.

It should be understood that the lines should be essentially parallel, and should, in the same general area of the chart, remain relatively equidistant. However, they *do not* have to remain equidistant if conditions change in a stock. They tend, in fact, to be somewhat closer together during rapid stock moves and further apart during congestion areas and turning points, as at areas marked 3.

The day marked 4 is especially important because it *forced* our lines to turn downward. There was no way we could sufficiently expand the width of our channel to encompass that day of trading and still maintain the upward slope of the trend. There had obviously been a dramatic change in the stock action. The subsequent two days of trading became a rally in the newly established downtrend and served to define the approximate width of the downward channel, just as the pullbacks, marked 1, had defined the width of the upward channel. Using that width as our new channel, we were then *forced* to curve upward at areas marked 5. It is this forcing of a change of direction that dictates the position of the channel.

When we outlined the minor wave, we compared it to a stream with its rapids, pools, and waterfalls. If that was the actual water in the stream, then the intermediate channel could be compared to the streambed, the areas where the overall stream is confined by sharper banks as it twists downhill. This done, we now need to map the river valley itself. This is the major pattern that we will work on next.

THE MAJOR WAVE

Our process in outlining the major wave is no different from that used in outlining the intermediate wave. We want to construct a pair of parallel lines that will come close to or touch the highs and lows of the waves of

Figure 9–4
AETNA—DAILY (interval: 50,000 shares; minor, intermediate, and major waves outlined)

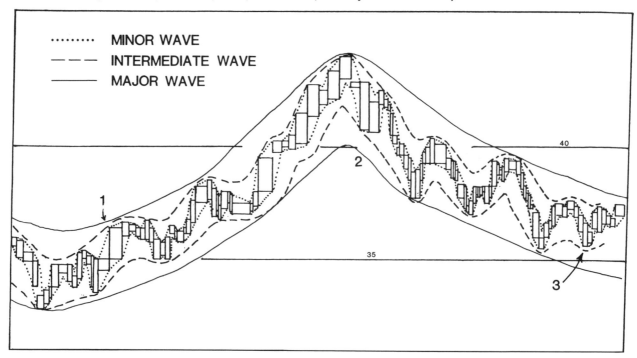

the intermediate channel. The lines should be as close together as possible, their width being dictated by the extent of the pullbacks during declines and the extent of the rallies during advances. We want to have smooth and fairly equidistant lines. They may widen or narrow somewhat, but may not diverge from one another. If a high occurs in the intermediate pattern which forces the upper line to turn up, the bottom line must also be turned up in the same way. On Figure 9–4, we can see that this happened at area 1. Similarly, if the intermediate wave drops enough to force the lower line to turn down, the upper line must be made to follow it as at point 2. As we go off the right side of the page, we continue the wave pattern downward, since that is all we know at that time, based upon this chart. The intermediate wave is up and is close to the upper limit of the major trend, but there has not (as yet, at least) been enough upward movement to cause us to curve the major channel back upward. Should the stock get much stronger, however, we would have to revise our lines and recognize a change of direction in the major trend. A hint that this might be happening is seen at point 3 where the intermediate wave did not return all the way to the lower limits of the channel we had assumed.

Perhaps, however, there is other information that will help us to see if the major channel is likely to turn up at this time. Maybe we are not seeing enough information. It appears in Figure 9–4 that we are seeing, at its center, the crest of a larger wave. Maybe, by looking at a longer-term picture, we will be able to identify an even larger pattern, one that will help us to predict the probable future direction of the major wave.

THE WEEKLY CHART

There are two ways to search out the larger patterns. One is to merely have more daily history, ending up with a daily-based chart which may spread across two walls. The other is to construct a chart with a smaller scale. We prefer the second solution. Figure 9–5 is a weekly chart of Aetna posted with a 300,000-share interval, whereas we used a 50,000-share interval for the daily chart. Each rectangle represents an entire week of trading, so the entire chart represents 82 weeks (more than a year and a half of trading). With this chart, perhaps we will be able to see not only the river, its bed, and its valley, but also determine in what general direction the river is flowing.

In order to properly analyze this chart, we will have to go through the same scaling up process we did in the daily chart. We will start at the minor wave, go to the intermediate wave, and finish at the major wave. It should be realized that these will be different waves, with different names. We are treating this as a new chart and will follow the same rules we must follow with every chart. The result, as we will see later, is that the intermediate wave on the daily chart becomes the minor wave on the weekly chart, the major wave on the daily chart becomes the intermediate wave on the weekly chart, and we are able to isolate another, larger wave on the weekly chart.

In Figure 9–5, we have outlined the minor wave pattern, using the same system of connecting the box corners. As we would expect, since we are looking at longer-term information, these lines tend to be more regular and parallel than the minor wave on a daily chart. Again, we see some narrowing in accelerated up or down moves and some widening in congestion areas and turning points, but it is less pronounced. The cycle we have outlined is the same cycle we called the intermediate cycle on the daily-based chart.

From here, we move on to the next chart (Figure 9–6) on which we have, following the same rules, delineated the intermediate trend within dashed lines. This cycle is the same as the major trend we found on the daily-based charts. Looking at the entire chart, rather than just the area covered originally on the daily-based chart, we can see that we were, as we suspected, looking at just one wave in a much larger pattern. This pattern should help to indicate what we might be able to expect from the stock on a longer-term basis. To do this, though, we still must follow the rules and draw in the next larger channel. We have done this on Figure 9–7.

The major trend we have determined in Figure 9–7 is a new one. It was too big for us to have been able to recognize it on the daily chart. It seems to be telling us that the pullback was only to the bottom of the major channel, and that the general direction of the stock is still up.

With this information, our remaining worry is the possibility that the

Figure 9–5
AETNA—WEEKLY (interval: 300,000 shares; minor waves outlined)

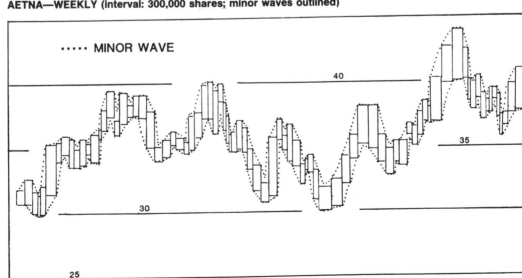

Figure 9–6
AETNA—WEEKLY (interval: 300,000 shares; minor and intermediate waves outlined)

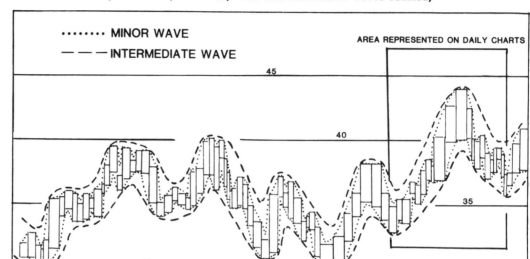

stock may penetrate the level and turn the major trend down. Going back to the daily-based chart, however, we can see that the *daily-based* major has begun to turn upward. It appears that the long-term move is still intact and that prices should advance from this level.

As can be seen from the foregoing discussion, outlining the various wave patterns and recognizing changes of direction in each wave can be a very worthwhile trading tool. A trader should be aware of the direction of each wave pattern and never go against the trend of the wave he is trading. Further-

Figure 9–7
AETNA—WEEKLY (interval: 300,000 shares; minor, intermediate, and major waves)

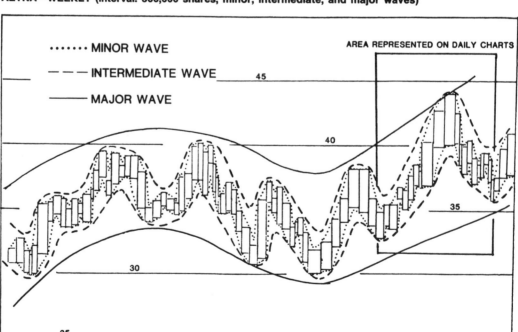

more, he should also know the larger wave patterns that may curtail or enhance the performance of the wave he is trading. The final chapters of this book will go further into the utilization of wave patterns, combined with all of the other techniques covered in order to demonstrate how to trade successfully.

As we have delineated each pattern of waves in these charts, it should have become apparent to the reader that there seems to be a regularity to these waves. This regularity is the primary point toward which we have been working. The next chapter demonstrates how one should recognize the waves, measure them, and use them as a predictive tool.

Chapter 10   Wave Patterns on Daily Charts

Imagine yourself driving over a bumpy country road in a car with bad shock absorbers. Every rock and ripple in the road causes a small bounce. The road is, in fact, washboarded, so that there is a regular up-and-down vibration. The shaking is irritating, certainly, but has no real effect upon the direction of the car as it travels over the road. From time to time, however, there are bumps and potholes, which cause much more violent bounces. They tend to make driving difficult and shake the car a good deal, but even they are not really affecting the uphill or downhill progress of the car. The hills and valleys, on the other hand, are significant. They change the overall direction of the car. The car strains as it climbs the hills, tops the hills, and then coasts down into the valleys. All the time, it is being shaken by the washboard and bounced by the potholes.

There is an even more significant longer-term direction to your drive than the hills and valleys, however. Maybe the trip is from the plains, through the foothills, and up into the mountains. Perhaps it is the reverse, from the mountains down into the plains.

The action of a stock is much like your bumpy automobile ride. The shaking ripples on the road are the rhythmic minor bumps on our charts, the pattern outlined by the minor wave lines. Every small pebble can cause a shake, but it does not change the direction of travel. In a stock, these pebbles and ridges are influences that cause price fluctuation. The internal factors may be such diverse factors as a large holder who needs to raise money to pay his taxes, or a bank trust department that is restructuring a portfolio. They are the result of thousands of individual decisions to buy or sell the stock that have little or nothing to do with the market's basic evaluation of the value of the stock.

External factors contributing to the ripple pattern could be news items about the industry, fluctuations in the overall market, specialist actions, or any number of other factors. The important point is that the overall direction of the stock is unaffected.

The next larger pattern, the potholes and bumps in the road, translates to the intermediate wave pattern on our daily-based chart. This is the more significant because there is enough movement here for the trader to use it as a money-making tool. It is caused, in the stock, by more dramatic changes in the public attitude toward the stock, and to the stock market. As in all stock moves, the potholes are a result of the public evaluation of every item that can change the supply-demand equilibrium. It can be affected by earnings reports or estimates, newspaper articles, contract awards, government actions, international news, presidential pronouncements, general market conditions, money markets, and so forth. As with the ripples, however, these potholes are only large bounces, and do not change the overall direction in which the car is traveling. Where our analogy falls down is on the country road— we never know where the next pothole will be. In a stock, the potholes seem to be spaced very evenly, so evenly as to make them quite predictable.

Next, we have the hills and valleys, the major wave on our daily-based chart. These are the longer-term trends, reflecting the public's attitude toward the future prospects of this company. They also are affected by external factors such as overall market conditions, but are much more independent of such influences. They are the rhythmic waves of the stock, in a large part a function of the passing of the float from strong hands to weak hands and back to strong hands. These are the waves that can be profitable for the longer-term investor rather than just the short-term trader. They can last many weeks or months, and present possible gains of 10 to 30 percent or more.

Finally, we have the overall landscape. Are we going into the mountains or out of the mountains? These are the super wave patterns on our daily charts, the major wave on our weekly charts. They are the trends that may last for years. They represent the long-term public attitude toward the stock, its industry and the overall economy. These trends serve two purposes. First, they provide the limits we can expect for the swings in our major wave pattern, and second, they provide the necessary information for very long-term buy-and-hold investors.

There is another factor in our automobile-and-road analogy which emerges, and it may help to relate the role of volume in our cyclical studies. The speed at which we drive is a direct function of the quality of the road. If there are more bumps and hills, we tend to go slower. If it is a·smooth, well-graded highway, we tend to drive faster. On a backcountry road we may drive at 20 miles per hour, because the road rises and drops over many hills and valleys. On the super highway the bulldozers and graders have removed all the minor hills, so we go 60.

But at 20 on the back road we may top a hill every three minutes because they are each one mile apart. On the super highway, we only top a hill every three miles rather than every mile, but we still top a hill every three minutes, because we are going 60 miles an hour rather than 20.

So it is with a stock. At high speed (heavy volume) we may make an intermediate low every 5 days, while at low speed (light volume) we may make that low every 10 days. The lower volume makes us stretch out the time needed to reach each valley.

Equivolume charts, with their volume-based X-axis, vary their speed across the page as volume changes. They make it possible to measure the distance between the hills and valleys, regardless of the speed we are driving, and compensate for the quality of the highway.

THE MINOR WAVE PATTERN

Let us look at Figure 10–1. Here we have a daily-based chart of General Motors, covering about four months of trading during 1981. The volume interval is 100,000 shares since this is a heavily traded stock. We have already drawn in the dotted line minor wave pattern and the dashed line intermediate wave pattern. We are going to be studying only the minor wave pattern at this time, but we must have the intermediate pattern drawn in, in order to better recognize the minor waves. *Always* outline the next larger wave pattern than the one you are interested in interpreting. Only in this way can you tell the difference between the ripples and the potholes.

The steps in recognizing the waves in the minor pattern are as follows:

1. Mark each area where the minor wave touches or approaches the intermediate wave.

Figure 10–1
GENERAL MOTORS—DAILY (interval: 100,000 shares)

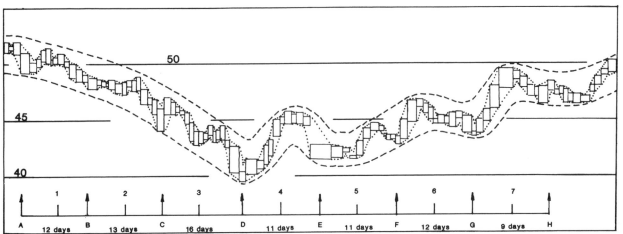

2. Observe the rhythmic pattern.
3. Mark the most prominent low, measure laterally to the next significant low. Continue this measurement, noting the slight differences in distance. Then adjust the measurement to approximately fit all of the significant troughs in the minor wave.

We have done this in Figure 10–1, marking each low in the minor wave with a letter. Point D was the most important low, from which we worked both left and right. Point C was obviously a prominent low which helped us to recognize the pattern. The F–G distance also helped to confirm this wave pattern. Point E is a part of a broad low area, making it hard to point out the exact low, except through the implications of the minor wave pattern. Point B is a low, but the slight rise beyond it is only a minor hesitation in the strong downward move. At C, the stock was still very weak and could only support a feeble rally. The strong rally between D and E indicated a change in the trading nature of the stock, which was confirmed by the higher low at E. Point F, again a higher low, right where we would expect it, added to our conviction that there had been a change of direction in the stock, which was justified by the continuing strength in each subsequent wave.

It should be noted that we are using lows rather than highs in measuring the cycles. Low points on stocks seem to occur in a more regular manner. The lows are a function of the constant available float, so that approximately the same number of shares changes hands in each full cycle. The highs are less reliable, since they are indicating the strength of weakness of a stock. The high moves to the right during periods of strength, since more stock is accumulated on the rise than is distributed on the subsequent decline.

In a weak stock, the highs tend to move to the left as more stock is distributed than was accumulated. Figure 10–2 shows the wave pattern we have recognized in the General Motors chart (Figure 10–1). It can be seen that the lows, A through H, are very regular, providing us with a worthwhile predictive tool. The highs are much more erratic, however, and are harder to pinpoint. Lows on charts tend to be recognizable points, since they are usually quite sharp, while highs tend to be rounded and therefore less well defined.

The position of the tops is often providing us with additional information. They move to the left during declines and to the right during advances, thus helping to show us turning points in the next larger wave pattern. The

52

Figure 10–2
MINOR WAVE PATTERN

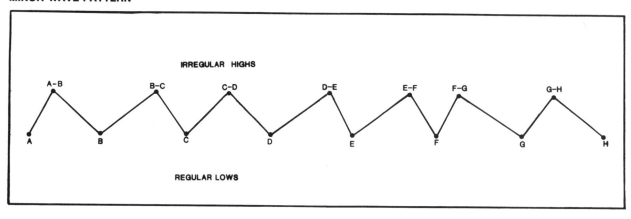

result is a tendency for the two tops that occur as a stock turns upward in the next larger pattern to be further apart than their normal interval. We have gone from a time of liquidation to a time of accumulation. The last cycle on the downmove shows more stock being sold than being bought, moving the top to the left. The next cycle, the first of the upmove, shows more stock being bought than being sold, moving the top to the right. This spreads the tops apart on the chart, as in tops C–D and D–E, indicating that the intermediate wave pattern is starting to turn up.

In Figure 10–1, there are some lows that were not as prominent as those we lettered A through H. These represent an even smaller wave pattern, a pattern which is a half-wave function of the minor wave pattern. These are usually too small for successful use, even by the most nimble trader, but should be recognized in order to avoid confusion and misinterpretation of the minor wave pattern. We have numbered these half-wave lows 1 through 7. This is a very sensitive pattern, and one that can be greatly affected by the action of the larger wave which contains it. At times, a stock can be strong enough or weak enough to make some of the points disappear. At point 4, for example, we see no evidence of a downward move. The stock was exhibiting such strength that the expected pullback was entirely erased. Perhaps if we had an hourly-based chart, rather than daily-based, this pullback would show itself, but on this chart it has completely disappeared.

Moving on to the next larger wave pattern, we have, in Figure 10–3, drawn in the major wave channel. We must have this in order to recognize the intermediate waves. As before, we mark those low points where the intermediate wave touches or approaches the major wave line. They have been shown, across the top of the chart, as numbers one through six. Low #3 was the most prominent, and the pattern to lows 4, 5, and 6 was easily recognized. Low #1 is also evident, but #2 is hardly evident at all. The stock was in a sharp decline, so no real rally came in to define point #2.

Looking at Figure 10–4, we see that the lows are again extremely regular, but the tops are far less reliable. The relationship of B–C and C–D has moved to the right.

In the next chapter we will again look at General Motors, utilizing the weekly chart, but first let us study another daily chart. Figure 10–5 shows the price and volume action of Allis Chalmers in early 1981. For this less active stock we have used a 10,000-share interval in our postings. Wherever the minor wave pattern has neared the intermediate wave we have shown a minor cycle low. These are lettered A through I. As in the General Motors example, one can also discern a half-wave pattern between these points. Since the stock was in a general downtrend, some of the rallies are very weak, as

Figure 10–3
GENERAL MOTORS—DAILY (interval: 100,000 shares)

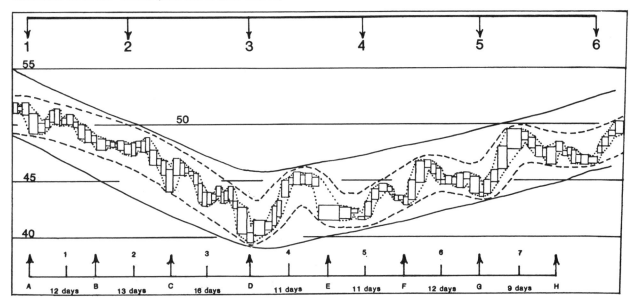

in E–F, but all the cycles are well represented. Also, as in the prior example, we see a spreading of the tops in the F–G and G–H areas, indicating the larger cycle may be turning to the upside.

Since the stock is obviously moving down, a trader utilizing the minor wave, perhaps for trading options, should not try to play the rallies. They will be feeble, and may be short-lived. He should only use the short side if the next larger cycle points downward. This can be treated as a basic rule in cycle trading: *Only go with the moves which are in the direction of the next larger cycle.* In a stock which shows an intermediate cycle in an *up*move, never try to utilize the declines in the minor cycle for short positions. Use this stock only for long positions until the next larger cycle tells you otherwise. (More on trading techniques in the final section of this book.)

Moving to the next illustration (Figure 10–6), we see the same stock with the major wave outlined, allowing us to study the intermediate pattern. Points A, B, and C are very obvious and almost exactly equidistant. Judging by these waves, it would appear that point D should occur just beyond the edge of the chart. The stock has already started down toward the lower major trend line but has not yet reached it. Since the stock, based upon

Figure 10–4
INTERMEDIATE WAVE PATTERN

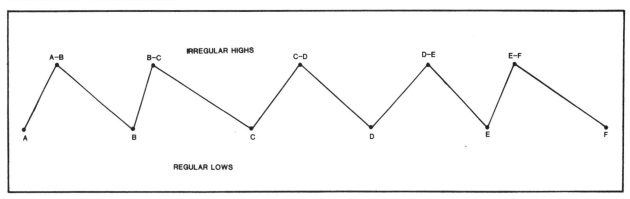

Figure 10–5
ALLIS CHALMERS—DAILY (interval: 10,000 shares minor and intermediate waves outlined)

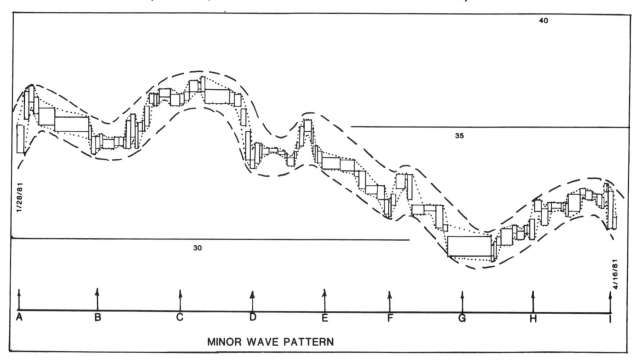

MINOR WAVE PATTERN

Figure 10–6
ALLIS CHALMERS—DAILY (interval: 10,000 shares; major, intermediate, and minor waves outlined)

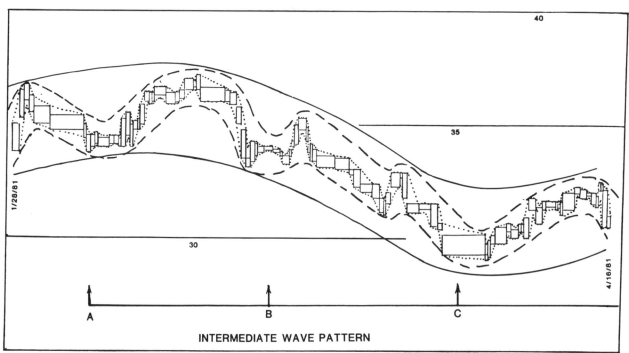

INTERMEDIATE WAVE PATTERN

the fact that the rally after C has curved the major trend upward, is apparently changing to an uptrend, we would be willing to go to the long side if:

1. We reach the lower trend line.
2. The cycle predicts a low.
3. There is a sign of bottoming, such as as oversquare box followed by some strength.

It would be worthwhile, however, to consult a weekly chart to see if the major cycle is really due to turn up as appears on the daily chart. The next chapter deals with charts on a weekly basis.

Chapter 11   Wave Patterns on Weekly Charts

Our reasons for using weekly charts are twofold. First is the confirming value they add to the daily work. They provide a tool whereby the trader can make sure that he is not bucking a primary trend. It is extremely important that a trader be in phase with the stock. If it is in an uptrend, he should only be using it for long positions. If it is in a downtrend, he must resist the temptation to play the rallies, and only use it for short positions. A trader should never try to use the same stock in both directions, reversing from long to short positions on a signal. It takes one wave to indicate that a stock has changed its direction in the next larger pattern. Only after that happens should the stock be moved from the down category to the up category, or vice versa.

The second use of weekly charts is for longer-term investments. In this usage, the same methods are applied by the investor as would be applied by the trader using daily charts. As before, the trends should be outlined, using the scaling-up techniques in Chapter 9. Then the bottoms should be ascertained within each wave pattern, and projections of the next probable tops and bottoms should be made.

We have followed this procedure in Figure 11–1. This is a weekly chart of McDonald's Corporation during 1981 and part of 1982. Noticing when the minor wave dips toward the intermediate channel, we see that this is a very short cycle, usually lasting only about six weeks. These points have been labeled 1–12. This being a weekly chart, the points are not well defined in many cases. Perhaps a trader using a daily chart could utilize these swings, but they are too close together and poorly defined on the weekly chart to be of value to the longer-term investor.

The next larger wave, though, is very regular and certainly could be very helpful. We have marked, with the letters A, B, and C, the three points where the intermediate wave meets the major channel. They are about six months apart and represent substantial longer-term moves. In addition, there is an uptrend apparent in the major channel, indicating the stock should be used on the long side, not the short side. Beyond point C, the stock is moving upward well, toward the upper limits of the channel. It appears, however, that it is too late to be a buyer, as the stock goes off the right-hand margin. If the stock continues its cyclic pattern, it is well over 50 percent of the way through the cycle, implying that a corrective downward move is in the offing. The investor should wait for completion of the next decline, and, if the major channel has not turned down, buy the stock.

Let us go back now to General Motors (Figure 11–2), the stock we were studying on the daily charts in Chapter 10. We have indicated the area that was depicted on the daily charts. The upmove that was evident in the second half of the daily is very well outlined in the weekly. One would be

Figure 11–1
McDONALD'S CORPORATION—WEEKLY (interval: 150,000 shares)

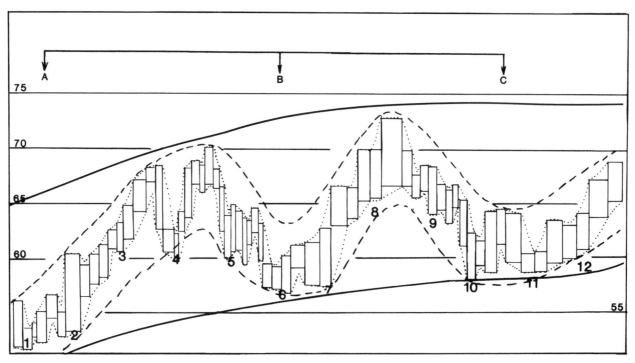

Figure 11–2
GENERAL MOTORS—WEEKLY (interval: 250,000 shares)

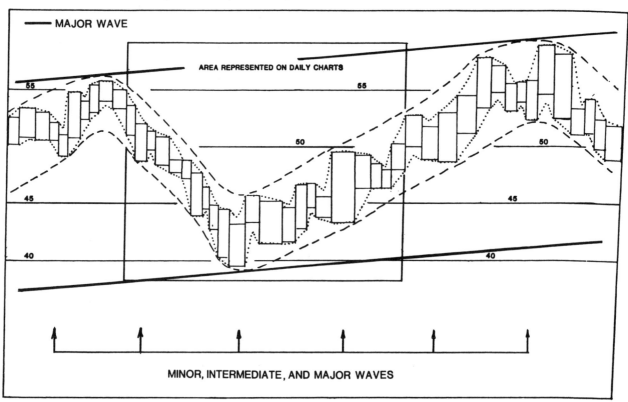

inclined to be a buyer each time the stock returns to the lower limits of the intermediate channel. The weekly chart also tells us something else: The major channel appears to be in a very long-term advance. This gives us another reason to be buying the stock and reinforces the conclusion that we should only be using this stock on the long side, at least for the time being.

Of particular importance is the fifth from the last week on this chart. In our drawing of the intermediate channel, it forces us to turn the lines down. The intermediate upward move appears to have ended, and we can see the possibility of a return to the lower limits of the major channel. By then, of course, we also know that a low on the minor cycle is due fairly soon, and that the intermediate cycle has passed the halfway point.

Weekly charts are valuable to the shorter-term trader, because they help to confirm his daily charts. For a longer-term investor, they are imperative. The longer-term, larger cycles are at least as reliable as the smaller cycles on the daily charts, and the moves represented are far larger and more profitable. They allow us to look at the long-term direction of a stock and protect us from buying on highs or selling on lows. The serious long-term investor should maintain a library of weekly charts from which to make his selections.

Chapter 12   Wave Patterns in the Market

The regularity we have observed in individual stocks also reflects itself in the overall market, and can be used as a predictive tool. We must realize, however, that the indices being used are formed by combining the prices and volumes of a large number of stocks, all of which have their own patterns which may or may not be in phase with one another. Even in the worst markets, some stocks are going up; and in the best of bull markets, many stocks are going down. So, when we are looking at a market average, we must be aware it is just that—an average.

There tends to be, as a result, a smoothing of both price and volume information. A very strong day in the market may move the Dow industrials up 3 percent, but many stocks may have jumped up 25 percent, while others did nothing. Similarly, we are startled if market volume increases 50 percent over the previous day, but are not particularly surprised if an individual issue triples its volume. The smoothing means that the moves are not likely to be as dramatic as those of individual issues, and turning points often will not be as sharp; but it does not mask the fact that there is a rhythm to the overall market—a rhythm which extends all the way from the small cycles, which last a few days, to the giant swings, which last a number of years.

Let us first look at a short period of daily information in Figure 12–1. We have outlined all three channels. It can be readily seen that the points at which the minor wave approaches the intermediate wave are very regular in terms of volume. Points 1, 2, 3, and 4 are evenly spaced and would allow us to project point 5. The volume on this chart is 10 million shares, making the marked low points about 700 million shares apart. The points are not as regular on a time basis: Points 1 and 2 are 10 days apart, points 2 and 3 are 14 days apart, and points 3 and 4 are 12 days apart. We also can see evidence of an intermediate low showing itself between each pair of these points.

Moving on to our weekly charts, we have illustrated a three-year period beginning in Figure 12–2 and continuing in Figure 12–3. We see here the bear market of 1976–77, followed by the beginning of a stronger market in 1978. Studying first the way in which the minor wave approaches the lower limits of the intermediate wave, we see a rhythm that is quite regular, with the dips 6 to 10 weeks apart. These are better recognized on a daily chart, however.

The more important information is transmitted by the points at which the intermediate wave approaches the major wave. We have numbered these 1 through 8. They are evenly enough spaced to provide a predictive tool, and would allow us to project the next logical buy point at 9. These swings

Figure 12–1
DOW JONES INDUSTRIALS—DAILY

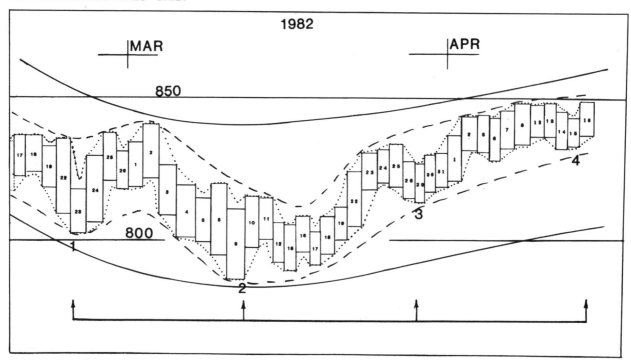

Figure 12–2
DOW JONES INDUSTRIALS—WEEKLY (1976–1977)

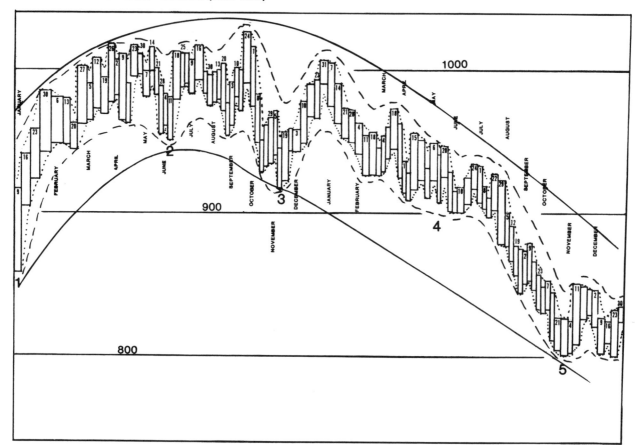

Figure 12–3
DOW JONES INDUSTRIALS—WEEKLY (1978)

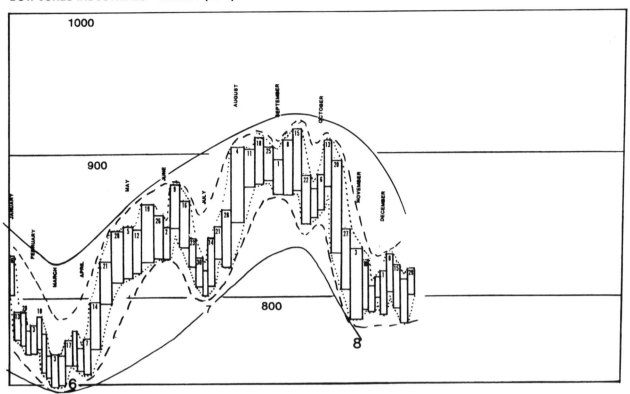

are far more than just market fluctuations. They last about six months and are likely to encompass market moves of 10 percent or more.

Finally, we move on to the monthly-posted Dow Jones industrials (Figure 12–4) and follow the same procedures of outlining and analysis. Now we are looking at more than five years of history, including the bull market top in early 1973, the disasterous bear market lasting into late 1975, and the subsequent skyrocketing rally. Here we can particularly see the features we point out in the stream analogy in Chapter 9. We can observe the widening of the stream in congestion areas and the narrowing during rapid moves. Especially apparent is the pool and waterfall effect during the bear market of 1973–74.

Observing when the minor wave approaches the lower limits of the intermediate channel, we see six distinct points, evenly spaced, which have been numbered in Figure 12–4. The only entry which could have caused confusion was point 3, which might, almost as logically, be assigned to the prior low, three months earlier. Here, then, is a wave pattern, one which encompasses years of trading and continues to show a rhythmic regularity like the heartbeat of the market.

If we can see ripples on the daily charts, waves on weekly charts, and great storms moving across the ocean on the monthly charts, would it be possible to find some logical tidal rhythms in the bull and bear markets which push and pull the market in moves that encompass many years? Certainly there can be little logic to these great shifts on a time basis. Looking at a time-based chart of the market going back to the turn of the century, we see significant market declines ending in 1932, 1938, 1942, 1962, 1966, 1970, 1974, 1978, 1980, and 1981 (see Figure 12–5). The time spans between them, then, are 6 years, 4 years, 20 years, 4 years, 4 years, 4½ years, 3½ years, 2 years, and 1½ years. There is little logic to these intervals. Looking

Figure 12–4
DOW JONES INDUSTRIALS—MONTHLY

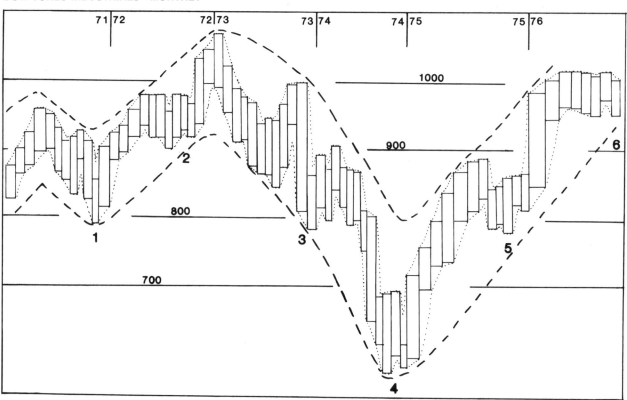

Figure 12–5
DOW JONES INDUSTRIALS—YEARLY (1900–1961; interval: 100,000,000 shares)

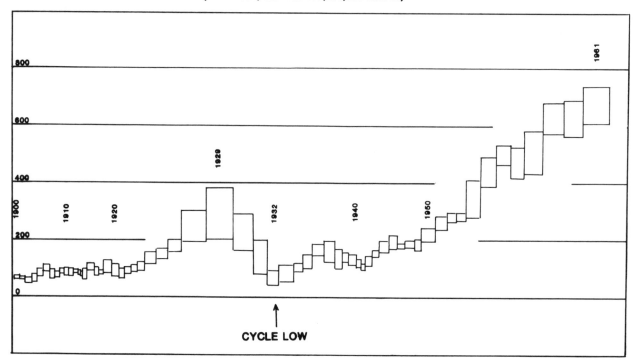

at the volume, however, a different pattern appears. If we can consider 1938 and 1942 as temporary pullbacks in a giant bull market which began in 1932 and finally ended with the 1961–62 decline, we have a 30-year full cycle. Adding the volume over that time span, we see that slightly over 15 billion shares were traded. From 1962 until 1970 (see Figure 12–6), a period of eight years, we see that over 16 billion shares changed hands. We have omitted the 1966 low, which was about a 50 percent retreat from the prior advance and not a true bear market. The next major full cycle in the market ended in 1974, a span of 4½ years, but again almost 16 billion shares changed hands in that time. It begins to appear that a pattern is emerging. The volume interval between bear market lows seems to remain fairly constant, but the period is getting shorter on each cycle because of the increasing volume of trading. The next cycle lasts a year less, 3½ years, but encompasses 17.5 billion shares, slightly more than the prior cycles, bringing us to the low in early 1978, after two years of general decline.

From 1978 to 1980, we again see 17.5 billion shares traded, as the market makes a sharp low in March of that year. The time interval has been shortened again, but volume has remained constant. It appears that the market has a regular rhythm in the 16–18 billion share range.

The last pattern at the time of this writing was the 1980–81 cycle. From a decline to the low 700s on the Dow, it rose to over the 1,000 level, only to decline sharply in 1981 to the 800 level. This full cycle lasted 17.9 billion shares in terms of volume, but only 19 months in terms of time.

Figure 12–6
DOW JONES INDUSTRIALS—YEARLY (1962–1981; interval: 400,000,000 shares; note scale change from prior chart)

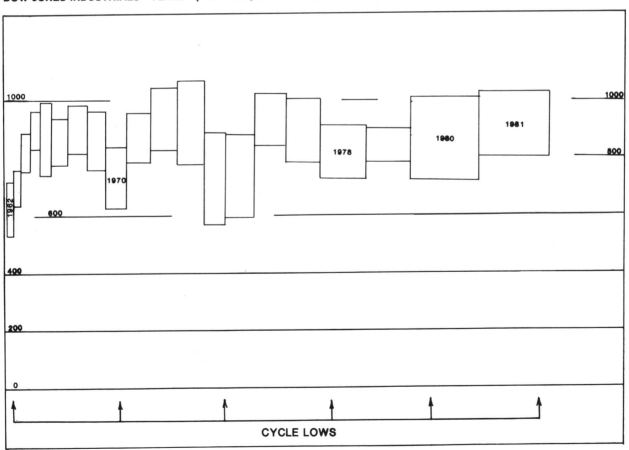

Why should the market exhibit such a regularity over so many years? If the number of shares in the marketplace had remained constant over those years, we would be able to ascribe it to the "float" being passed back and forth. This is certainly not the case. In 1932, there were fewer companies listed and far fewer shares. We can only observe the phenomenon, seeing the same pattern repeat six times, and accept it as an aid in forecasting future market moves. There appears to be a long-term heartbeat in the market which can only be described using a volume measurement.

Chapter 13   The Elliott Wave Modified

Probably the most fascinating piece of research ever done on market cyclicality was done by R. N. Elliott between 1934 and 1948. His books and market letters make fascinating reading and contain observations which fit in well with the volume thesis. He observed that there appears to be a repeating pattern of price action in the stock averages (and, to a lesser extent, in individual stocks) which can serve as a predictive tool. Each of his largest waves is broken down into smaller waves, and each of these into even smaller waves in a scaling-down process which he carried into even the hourly fluctuations of the market.

Elliott's basic pattern, which he believed was based on "Nature's laws," was an eight-leg pattern, consisting of three upwaves with intermediate pullbacks, followed by two downwaves divided by one intermediate rally (see Figure 13–1). Superimposed on these waves is a similar pattern, breaking each rising wave down in the same way so that the major wave, ideally, should look like Figure 13–2. The downwaves have a reversed pattern of two up and three down instead of three up and two down. From this point, Elliott goes into the many variations to these rules, which help to explain waves that do not conform to the idealized pattern. He also shows the way in which straight-line channels can be drawn, helping to identify each wave.

We highly respect Elliott's work as a benchmark in technical analysis. He found patterns and predictability based upon the action of the market, rather than randomness based upon fundamentals. His recognition of the basic eight-leg pattern and his thesis of waves within waves fits in well with our view of the market. In light of our preoccupation with volume and our contention that market action is volume-based rather than time-based, we would make some modifications, however.

Two particular problems crop up when using Elliott's wave work. The first is when. Although he saw the waves and labeled them, they appear to be very irregular in their wave length, with one leg lasting a few weeks and another lasting many months. This leads to a confusion as to which wave pattern is really being studied. One often does not know if he is observing a pullback of smaller magnitude or a downleg in the larger pattern.

The second problem is the fact that Elliott described three upwaves followed by two downwaves as the standard pattern. If this were consistently true, it would give the market a long-term upward bias. It would move up more than it moved down.

Volume cyclicality may offer a solution to both of these problems. If we can identify volume cycles in the market, we may be able to differentiate between the different waves in accordance with their wave length, rather than their magnitude; and if we can slightly modify the wave theory, we may be able to eliminate the upward bias. We believe, as Elliott did, that

Figure 13–1
ELLIOTT WAVE

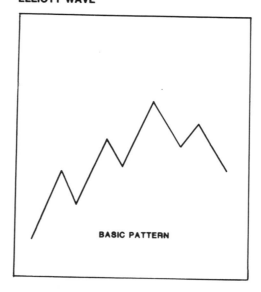

BASIC PATTERN

there is a reliable cyclicality to the market. But it is more than just a cycle; it is a rhythm, and that rhythm, the heartbeat of the market, is measured in volume.

The eight-leg pattern of Elliott's appears to us to be evident. We feel, however, that it is a pattern that is three legs up, two legs sideways, and three legs down, as shown in Figure 13–3.

The top is made up of two highs which ideally are the same, but which can vary so that one or the other can be higher. Now we have a symmetrical pattern that lends no bias to the market. Actually, the location of the highs and lows of each pattern will vary as they are influenced by an even larger wave pattern. We will come back, later in this chapter, to an actual example of this pattern, but first we will move on to the volume rhythm.

As we pointed out in Chapter 12, in the overall market there appears to be a very reliable cycle, which we have traced back to 1932. Let us take another look at these cycles, which have regularly repeated every 16–18 billion shares. Our lows were in 1932, 1962, 1970, 1974, 1978, 1980, and

Figure 13–2
ELLIOTT WAVE

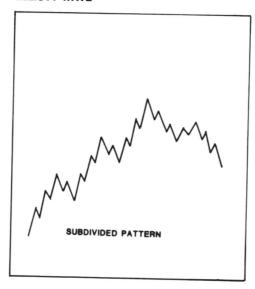

SUBDIVIDED PATTERN

Figure 13–3
MODIFIED WAVE

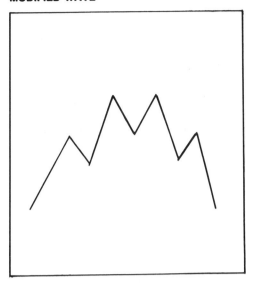

1981. Could it be that this is the super wave Elliott talks about? Figures 12–5 and 12–6 in the prior chapter show what could be interpreted as such a super wave, beginning in 1932 and ending in 1978. We have, indeed, a three-up pattern taking us to market highs in early 1973, and a two-down pattern coming to the market low in early 1978. The implication would be, then, that the 1978–80 wave was the first of a new super cycle, and the 1980–81 wave was the second. Now we are seeing not only a cycle, but a rhythm. Each major cycle is clearly defined by volume, giving us a far better predictive tool. If this is correct, then we would expect to be able to break

Figure 13–4
ONE MARKET CYCLE

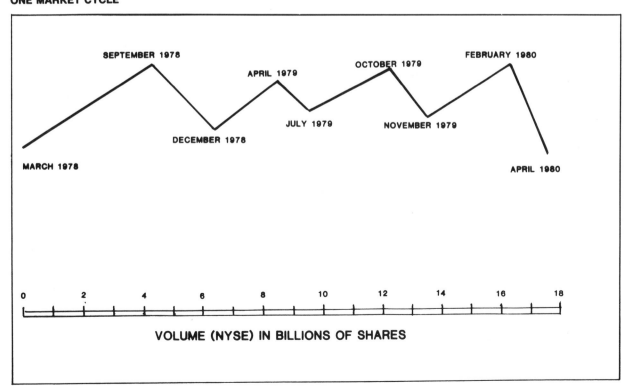

each of these major cycles into their components and have them also conform to the modified Elliott pattern.

Figure 13–4 is a volume-based simplified illustration of the 1978–80 market. We start with this cycle because it presents the pattern that comes closest to the ideal. One can see that all of the cycle bottoms are equidistant except the March–December 1978 cycle, which occupies about six billion shares, whereas the others are four billion shares apart. We have observed that often the first leg in a new bull market tends to be somewhat longer than the subsequent legs. In this example, all of the tops are at approximately the same level rather than the two middle tops being higher. We are seeing the eight-leg market that Elliott described, however.

Let us go back now to the 1932–62 cycle. Here we see a very regular pattern of tops and bottoms, based on volume. Since this was the first cycle of the new super cycle, the fourth top is higher than the second and third. The highs were made in 1936, 1946, 1956, and 1961. The lows were made in 1932, 1941, 1949, 1957, and finally in 1962. Again, we have a typical eight-leg cycle with fairly equidistant lows, in terms of volume.

The next cycle was 1962–70. There were three prominent tops—early 1966, mid-1967, and late 1968. As the market slid to 1970's low, there was a rally in late 1969, which would qualify as the fourth top and satisfy the modified Elliott requirements.

From 1970 to 1974 there was a dramatic cycle, with prominent tops in early 1971, early 1972, early 1973, and finally in early 1974. Between the 1973 and 1974 tops was another spike of short duration, which is hard to account for. The other parts of the cycle conform well to the idealized pattern.

From 1974–78, the cycle has a double top, much like our idealized cycle. The first leg, as expected, is longer. The final drop is interrupted by one brief rally, which makes the fourth top.

In the 1980–81 period, we have a dramatic example of how the time span of our cycles has been shortening. We are going through a volume cycle in less than 2 years, whereas it used to take 30 years to trade the same volume. This cycle has its highs in November 1980, January 1981, April 1981, and August 1981.

As we have seen in the previous chapter dealing with wave patterns in the overall market, there are very reliable cycles that show up in the daily, weekly, and monthly charts. These should show a correlation to the Elliott wave work, and in fact do. The cycle we were studying in the monthly charts of the Dow Jones industrials is the same cycle we have been looking at in breaking down the major legs of the modified Elliott super cycle. As we go below the monthly charts to the weekly charts, the Elliott method seems to break down, however. We have some cycles that can be divided into eight legs, while others have fewer or more legs yet conform well to the volume cyclicality. At the daily chart level, we see even less correlation to the Elliott wave. Each cycle, in this case, appears to have six legs rather than eight.

Our conclusion is that the Elliott wave, as modified, is most helpful in the largest cycles, but tends to become less helpful as we move to smaller and smaller wave patterns. Also, having tried to relate these cycles to individual issues rather than to the overall market, we find them not to be as helpful and prefer to deal with our cyclic studies on a scaling-up rather than a scaling-down basis. The larger moves, be they in individual stocks or in the overall market, are made up of many smaller moves. By scaling up, we take advantage of the waves that are tradeable, and read the larger moves as they develop.

Part Three   Ease of Movement

Chapter 14   Ease of Movement—The Objectives

Sitting on my side patio on a summer evening, I can look up and see a sky full of stars. Knowing a little bit about the heavens, I can pick out Orion, Cassiopeia, and the Big Dipper. These formations of bright points of light provide a pathway from one to another. The Dipper points my sights to Polaris, and Polaris shows me the way to Cassiopeia.

An astronomer, gazing through his powerful telescope sees far more. What I see as a bright spot in Orion becomes for him a giant nebula. He observes the changing rhythm of the universe, the pulsars with their precise repetitive signals, the rotation of the galaxy, the expansion of the universe.

An astrophysicist is likely to look at that same sky and see measurable quantities. His concern is the dynamic reactions taking place at the cores of these stars, the splitting and combining of elements that cause the lights I can only gaze at with awe.

In the first part of this book, we studied the stock market with the naked eye, looking for the formations that would guide us to profits. Primarily, we were utilizing the same methods used in other forms of charting but applying them to equivolume.

In Part Two, we were playing the part of the astronomer, looking at the dynamic systems that were at work in stocks. Through our telescope we attempted to identify the rhythms of the market, the regular repetitive patterns that would bring order and logic to what appeared at first to be chaotic randomness.

In this, the third section of the book, we will play the part of the astrophysicist. We will look closely at the components that make up Equivolume, and attempt to quantify these components. Each entry will be torn apart and analyzed numerically.

As we have seen, the shape of each box on an Equivolume chart is telling us a story. It is defining the supply and demand balance for that stock on that day. The high shows the level at which sellers become more powerful than buyers; the low shows the level at which buyers become more powerful than sellers. The distance apart between the high and the low—the spread—indicates the amount of disagreement that exists between buyers and sellers. The number of shares that change hands—the volume—is a measure of the amount of trading interest that exists between the spread parameters. We have learned that a narrow trading range indicates a reluctance for a stock to move, whereas a wide trading range indicates easy movement.

These factors, in turn, become more meaningful when we relate them to their neighboring boxes. Is the stock up or down when it develops a very overwide entry? Is it part of a continuing move, or a reaction in the other direction? Is it happening after a long move or out of a consolidation area?

We see, then, that there are three important pieces of information presented to us by a single day of trading.

1. Ease of trading.
2. Direction of movement.
3. Magnitude of movement.

Our job is to place values on these factors and combine them in such a way as to have a reliable, logical, and usable number that represents each day of trading. It is this number which we call the ease of movement value, or EMV.

In the following chapters we will show the method for calculating the EMV and apply it to individual stocks, first on daily charts, then on weekly charts. We will then illustrate a method for normalizing these numbers so that we can compare one stock to another. Finally, we will see how the same work applies to the study of the overall market.

Chapter 15   Calculating Ease of Movement

BOX RATIO

The first step in the calculation of ease-of-movement numbers is the quantification of each box on our charts. We want to arrive at a numerical equivalent to the shape of the box. We are not interested in its size, only its comparative proportions, since this is the factor which defines how easy or hard it is for the stock to move.

The shape of any rectangle is a function of its height and width. If we multiply these two numbers, we get the area of the rectangle. If we divide them, we get the ratio. Since we want to evaluate the *shape* of the box, regardless of its size, we will use a ratio calculation.

$$\frac{\text{Box width}}{\text{Box height}} = \text{Box ratio}$$

Since the width is depicting volume and the height is depicting price range, our formula is

$$\frac{\text{Volume}}{\text{Range}} = \text{Box ratio}$$

We will deal first with the exact box ratio (BR), using the raw numbers, and then move on to a more simplified method.

Exact Box Ratio

Let us suppose that a stock trades at a high today of 22½ and a low of 21¾. The range would be ¾ of a point, or .75. If on the same day 14,200 shares changed hands, our box ratio would be

$$\frac{14,200}{.75} = 18,933$$

Heavier volume would produce a higher BR value. For example, if 25,000 shares have traded

$$\frac{25,000}{.75} = 33,333$$

From our Equivolume charts, we recall that a heavier volume with the same price range produces a wider box (going toward square or oversquare). A wider box represents difficulty of movement. Therefore *a higher box ratio indicates more difficult movement; a lower box ratio indicates easier movement.*

If volume were to stay the same (14,200 in our example) but the price range increased to, say 2¼ points, the BR would drop dramatically:

$$\frac{14,200}{2.25} = 6,311$$

The reader should realize that, since we are dealing with ratios, box *size* has no importance; only box *shape* matters. If both height and width are doubled, tripled, quartered, or halved, the box ratio will remain the same.

$$\frac{14,200}{.75} = 18,933 \quad \text{or} \quad \frac{28,400}{1.50} = 18,933$$

Table 15–1 shows the calculation of the exact box ratios for an actual stock, Bally Manufacturing, during the spring of 1982. This should be related to the Equivolume chart of the stock (Figure 15–1). It can be seen that the higher BRs relate to the more square days, the lower BRs to the days of easier movement.

Simplified Box Ratio

The exact box ratio takes a good deal of record keeping and calculation and produces large numbers which are somewhat hard to work with. There is an easier method, however, which we call the simplified box ratio. To make this calculation, we must go back to our Equivolume charts and use lines and columns rather than actual volume figures and actual price ranges. Instead of volume figures we will count the number of columns of volume, and instead of price range we will count the number of eighths of range.

Table 15–1
BALLY MANUFACTURING—EXACT BOX RATIOS

Date	High	Low	Range	Volume	Exact box ratio
4/15/82	29⅜	28⅝	.75	702	936
4/16/82	30⅛	29¼	.875	2,228	2,546
4/19/82	30½	29¾	.75	2,575	3,433
4/20/82	30⅛	29⅜	.75	1,072	1,429
4/21/82	30¼	29⅝	.625	1,682	2,691
4/22/82	30½	29⅝	.875	2,188	2,501
4/23/82	29⅞	29¼	.625	1,262	2,019
4/26/82	30¼	29½	.75	2,040	2,720
4/27/82	30⅜	29⅜	1.00	2,787	2,787
2/82/82	30⅛	29½	.625	1,121	1,794
4/29/82	30⅞	29¾	1.125	3,446	3,063
4/30/82	31¼	30⅜	.875	3,211	3,670
5/03/82	30¾	30⅜	.625	1,282	2,051
5/04/82	30⅞	30½	.375	1,511	4,029
5/05/82	30⅝	29⅝	1.00	1,315	1,315
5/06/82	30⅝	29¾	.875	1,794	2,050
5/07/82	30¼	29¾	.50	1,391	2,782
5/10/82	29⅝	29⅛	.50	735	1,470
5/11/82	30⅛	29¼	.875	2,284	2,610
5/12/82	30	29½	.50	1,639	3,278
5/13/82	29¾	29⅛	.625	1,015	1,624
5/14/82	29¼	28⅞	.375	1,023	2,728
5/17/82	28⅞	28½	.375	1,513	4,035
5/18/82	28¾	28⅜	.375	807	2,152
5/19/82	28⅞	28⅜	.50	1,031	2,062
5/20/82	28⅝	27½	1.125	2,246	1,996
5/21/82	27⅞	27½	.375	949	2,531
5/24/82	27¾	27½	.250	1,316	5,264
5/25/82	28¼	27⅝	.625	2,097	3,355
5/26/82	27⅞	27	.875	1,758	2,009
5/27/82	27¼	26⅜	.875	1,323	1,512
5/28/82	26¾	26⅜	.375	773	2,061
6/01/82	26¾	26¼	.50	940	1,880
6/02/82	27⅛	26⅜	.75	1,480	1,973
6/03/82	27¼	26¾	.50	991	1,982

Figure 15–1
BALLY MANUFACTURING—DAILY (1982; interval: 50,000 shares)

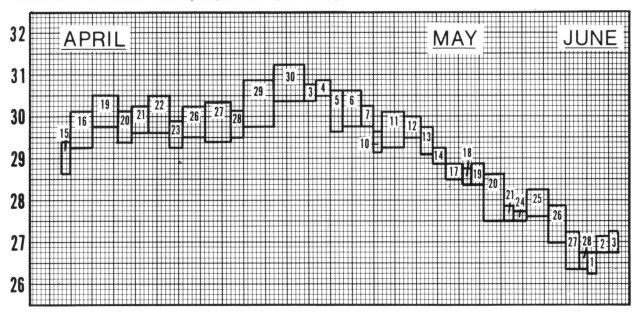

In Figure 15–2, we see Equivolume entries of various sizes and shapes. A is a fairly normal day of trading. The width of the rectangle is five columns, while the height is eight lines. Therefore the simplified box ratio is

$$\frac{\text{Width}}{\text{Height}} = \frac{5}{8} = .63$$

B is an oversquare day with a volume of 12 columns and a range of 6 lines. Therefore the box ratio is

$$\frac{12}{6} = 2.00$$

Both C and D are the same width as their height (5 by 5 and 10 by 10), so both have the same value of 1.00 even though they are of different sizes.

E is a day in which the stock moved very easily. It has a width of only 3 columns and a height of 13 lines. Therefore the BR is .23. As we saw in the exact BR work, the lower the BR value the easier the movement.

Now we have a BR which is much easier to work with and which can be quickly derived directly from our Equivolume charts, eliminating the need

Figure 15–2

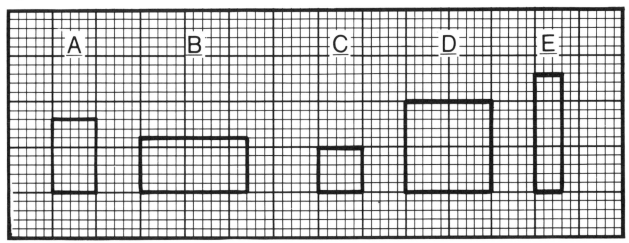

Figure 15–3
BALLY MANUFACTURING—DAILY (1982; interval: 50,000 shares)

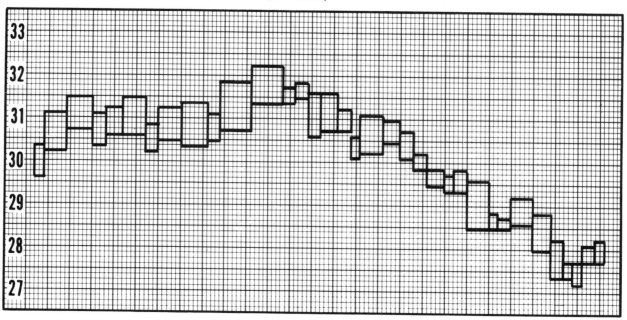

Table 15–2
BALLY MANUFACTURING—SIMPLIFIED BOX RATIO

Date	Volume	Range	Simplified box ratio
4/15/82	2	6	.333
4/16/82	5	7	.714
4/19/82	6	6	1.00
4/20/82	3	6	.50
4/21/82	4	5	.80
4/22/82	5	7	.714
4/23/82	3	5	.60
4/26/82	5	6	.833
4/27/82	6	8	.75
4/28/82	3	5	.60
4/29/82	7	9	.778
4/30/82	7	7	1.00
5/03/82	3	5	.60
5/04/82	4	3	1.333
5/05/82	3	8	.375
5/06/82	4	7	.571
5/07/82	3	4	.75
5/10/82	2	4	.50
5/11/82	5	7	.714
5/12/82	4	4	1.00
5/13/82	3	5	.60
5/14/82	3	3	1.00
5/17/82	4	3	1.333
5/18/82	2	3	.667
5/19/82	3	4	.75
5/20/82	5	9	.556
5/21/82	2	3	.667
5/24/82	3	2	1.50
5/25/82	5	5	1.00
5/26/82	4	7	.571
5/27/82	3	7	.429
5/28/82	2	3	.667
6/01/82	2	4	.50
6/02/82	3	6	.50
6/03/82	2	4	.50

Table 15–3
BALLY MANUFACTURING—EXACT AND SIMPLIFIED BOX RATIOS

Date	Exact box ratio	Simplified box ratio	Exact box ratio normalized	Simplified box ratio normalized
4/15/82	93,600	.333	.379	.454
4/16/82	254,600	.714	1.03	.973
4/19/82	343,300	1.00	1.39	1.36
4/20/82	142,900	.50	.579	.681
4/21/82	269,100	.80	1.09	1.09
4/22/82	250,100	.714	1.01	.973
4/23/82	201,900	.60	.818	.817
4/26/82	272,000	.833	1.10	1.13
4/27/82	278,700	.75	1.13	1.02
4/28/82	179,400	.60	.727	.817
4/29/82	306,300	.778	1.24	1.06
4/30/82	367,000	1.00	1.49	1.36
5/03/82	205,100	.60	.831	.817
5/04/82	402,900	1.333	1.63	1.82
5/05/82	131,500	.375	.533	.511
5/06/82	205,000	.571	.831	.778
5/07/82	278,200	.75	1.13	1.02
5/10/82	147,000	.50	.596	.681
5/11/82	261,000	.714	1.06	.973
5/12/82	327,800	1.00	1.33	1.36
5/13/82	162,400	.60	.658	.817
5/14/82	272,800	1.00	1.11	1.36
5/17/82	403,500	1.333	1.64	1.82
5/18/82	215,200	.667	.872	.909
5/19/82	206,200	.75	.836	1.02
5/20/82	199,600	.556	.809	.753
5/21/82	253,100	.667	1.03	.909
5/24/82	526,400	1.50	2.13	2.04
5/25/82	335,500	1.00	1.36	1.36
5/26/82	200,900	.571	.814	.778
5/27/82	151,200	.429	.613	.584
5/28/82	206,100	.667	.835	.909
6/01/82	188,000	.50	.762	.681
6/02/82	197,300	.50	.800	.681
6/03/82	198,200	.50	.803	.681

for extensive record keeping. Figure 15–3 shows the same stock we worked with earlier (Bally), but on lined paper so that the columns and lines can be counted. The first entry, for example, is two wide by five high, giving us a value of .40. The next is five wide by seven high, for a value of .71. Table 15–2 shows the calculated simplified box ratios for the entire chart.

Since we have rounded up on volumes in our charting technique and are merely counting columns for the simplified BR, we know that the BR values will not be as precise. Let us compare the results, to see how much they digress. In Table 15–3, we have listed the exact box ratios in column two and the simplified box ratios in column three. In order to compare them, we averaged the exact box ratios and divided each entry by the average. This result is shown in column four. We then did the same with the simplified box ratios and listed them in column five. By comparing column four and column five, we see that the simplified box ratios are extremely similar to the exact box ratios. Although there is some variation, we feel that for our purposes in the ensuing work, the simplified box ratios are satisfactory.

THE MIDPOINT MOVE (MPM)

Now that we have arrived at a numerical evaluation of each Equivolume entry, the next step is the quantification of price movement and direction. Looking at prices in the newspaper, we find that the final column is usually the net change for the day. We feel that this number is not a valid way of measuring price movement. Let us suppose that a stock trades today between 72 and 74, finally closing at 72. Tomorrow it trades between 71 and 73 closing at 72½. On an Equivolume chart, it is quite obvious that the two days represent a downward bias to the stock. The closes, however, would indicate an upward move, since the close, day-to-day, was half a point higher. (See Figure 15–4.)

We prefer, therefore, to look at the midpoint move (MPM) of the stock. We assume that the center of the trading range better indicates which way the stock really is moving.

The midpoint is merely the sum of the high and the low divided by 2:

$$\frac{\text{Day's high} + \text{day's low}}{2} = \text{Midpoint}$$

We then compare the midpoint of each day to the midpoint of the day before. The result is a number with a positive or negative sign. Let us look at the history of a stock.

High	Low	Midpoint (MP) $\left(\dfrac{\text{High} + \text{Low}}{2}\right)$	Midpoint move (MPM) (Today's MP— Yesterday's MP)
41.25	40	40.625	
42	41	41.5	+ .875
42.25	41	41.625	+ .125
43.5	42.5	43	+1.375
43	42	42.5	− .500
42.5	42	42.25	− .250

As with the box ratio, there is a simpler way to do this, using the chart directly. We mark the midpoint of each box and then count the number of lines the price has moved. In that way we are expressing the move in squares (eighths) rather than points.

Repeating graphically the above example, we have the Equivolume chart on Figure 15–5. We have inserted a line in the center of each box to indicate the midpoint. The midpoint move is arrived at by counting the number of lines up or down between the small center lines of consecutive boxes.

EASE OF MOVEMENT VALUE (EMV)

Having arrived at the box ratio and the midpoint move, we are now ready to do the ease-of-movement value calculation. The MPM gives us the movement, while the BR give us the ease. All we need to do is combine them

Figure 15–4
UP DAY?

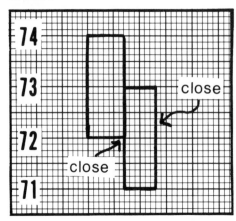

Figure 15–5

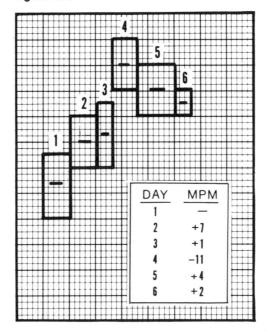

DAY	MPM
1	—
2	+7
3	+1
4	−11
5	+4
6	+2

into one number. Since an oversquare day indicates difficult movement, we would like to adjust the amount of movement in such a way that the amount of movement becomes less important when the entry is more square. On the other hand, if we have easy movement we would like to emphasize that day, giving it more importance. We accomplish this by taking the midpoint move and dividing it by the box ratio.

$$\frac{MPM}{BR} = EMV$$

In Figure 15–6, we show the price movement and the midpoints of a few days of stock history, then in Table 15–4 we have tabulated this data and arrived at the EMV for each day. Let us look at day one, the first rectangle on the chart and the first entry in the table. The volume of trading produced an entry five columns wide. The price range (high 28⅛, low 27) produced an entry nine lines high. By dividing the volume measurement by the range measurement (5÷9), we arrive at the box ratio of .56. Since this is the first entry, we have no knowledge as to whether this midpoint is higher or lower than the preceding day. We can mark the midpoint of this

Figure 15–6

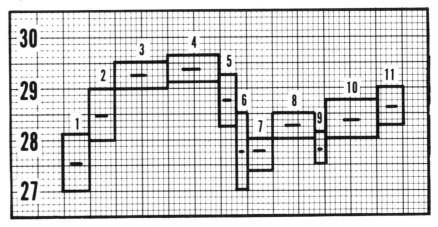

Table 15–4
EASE OF MOVEMENT VALUES

Day	Volume	Range	Box ratio	Midpoint move (MPM)	Ease of movement (EMV)
1	5	9	.56		
2	5	8	.63	+7.5	+11.9
3	10	4	2.50	+6.0	+ 2.4
4	10	4	2.50	+1.0	+ 0.4
5	3	8	.38	−5.0	−13.2
6	2	12	.17	−8.0	−47.1
7	5	5	1.00	−0.5	− 0.5
8	8	4	2.00	+4.5	+ 2.3
9	2	5	.40	−3.5	− 8.8
10	10	6	1.67	+4.5	+ 2.7
11	5	6	.83	+2.0	+ 2.4

box, however. The total range was nine lines, so the midpoint is 4½ lines up from the bottom of the box.

The second entry is five wide and eight high, so the BR is ⅝ = .63. Since the box is eight lines high, we can place the midpoint of the box up four lines (8÷2) from the bottom of the entry. Now, looking at this midpoint, we can compare it to the prior midpoint and see that there has been an upward move, midpoint to midpoint, of 7½ lines. Consequently, our entry in the MPM column is +7.5. Now we are ready for the first ease-of-movement-value calculation. We divide the midpoint move, +7.5, by the box ratio, .63, and get an EMV of +11.9. The original value of the upmove, +7.5, has been accentuated because the day was one of fairly easy movement. The new value for the day, +11.9, reflects the fact that the stock was finding little trouble moving up.

Day three is quite different, as we can see on the Equivolume chart. The stock is still moving up, but doing so grudgingly. The over-square day is showing that volume has gotten heavy, but progress is becoming difficult. It is an up day, but not an encouraging advance. There is too much volume in proportion to the price range. Our EMV calculation should therefore deemphasize that day.

Looking at the calculation, we see that the heavy volume (10) and the small range (4) produces a high BR of 2.50 (10÷4). The midpoint move was +6.0. Dividing the MPM by the BR:

$$6.0 \div 2.5 = +2.4$$

The day has been downgraded because of the high BR.

This tendency is even more pronounced on day four. The BR is again 2.50 and the MPM is only +1 line. Consequently, the EMV is only +.4. The stock has run into very heavy supply. By contrast, the next two days, during which the stock is declining, indicate ease of movement to the downside. Both box ratios are low (.38 and .17), showing that the stock is finding little support and is dropping on what selling is coming in. These are important moves, and should be emphasized. The calculation of the EMV does just that. The five-line point drop becomes a −13.2 and the eight-line drop becomes −47.1. The subsequent entries show the same tendency toward easy movement on the downside and difficult movement on the upside.

Chapter 16   Ease of Movement on Daily Charts

Having now determined the ease-of-movement value (EMV) for each day of trading, we need a way of utilizing these numbers. Our objective is to develop a trading tool that will numerically tell us when to buy and when to sell a particular stock. It should be sensitive enough to get us in at or near the beginning of a move, and should keep us in for the bulk of the move. Ideally, it should not produce whipsaws, which cost commissions without producing profits, and should recognize moves that are large enough to show worthwhile profits after paying commissions.

The signals should be clear-cut, eliminating guesswork. Additionally, we would like the signals to express magnitude. That is, there should be a difference between strong signals and weak signals, allowing us, in following many stocks, to select those that look most attractive at a time when a number of them generate a buy or sell signal simultaneously. EMV numbers, properly used, can do all of the above.

The size of the simplified EMV numbers can vary greatly from stock to stock. These variations are a function of two factors. First is the scaling of our charts. A high-priced stock plotted on a large vertical scale will produce large EMV numbers because each entry on the chart is depicted with a wide trading range. If, in addition, we are using a high number of shares as our volume increment, most days will be tall, thin rectangles. The result will be large EMV numbers. Conversely, if we have used a smaller number as our volume increment, the rectangles will be wider, giving lower EMVs. So, the way in which we plot our chart will, in itself, affect the size of the numbers with which we are working. This can be avoided by attempting to scale our charts so that neither the horizontal nor vertical dimensions are overemphasized.

The second variable is the volatility of the stock being plotted. A highly volatile stock will produce more dramatic moves and, hence, larger EMV values. This is not a drawback. Volatility, if we make the right decisions, is an asset. Profits are larger and quicker.

We have experimented with a large number of different moving averages of the EMV values in order to determine the most effective trading tool. A very short moving average, such as the three-day moving average, has the advantage of being in at the beginning of a move. It is extremely sensitive, needing only a small amount of strength to generate a buy signal. This very sensitivity, however, causes it often to mistake a fluctuation for the beginning of a move. It is interesting that the sensitivity of the three-day is such that it almost always is correct, on a very short-term basis. It comes in so early in a move that the move usually has further to go. Many of the moves are too small for a reasonable profit, using the underlying stock, but not too small for an extremely nimble options trader. It also will be the most prompt indicator at the beginning of a major move, and will thereby maximize profits. Its other attribute, a very important one, is the protection it provides. If the trader has entered a bad position, he is told to close it out before it has gone very far against him.

The drawbacks are also a result of the same sensitivity. A one-day feeble reversal is able to give a false signal, causing the trader to close out a position before a major move has gone to completion. He could, of course, reinstitute the position as soon as the three-day EMV swings back, but he will have paid two extra commissions. With a stock in a long sideways move, small buy-and-sell signals, with little meaning and less profit, can be repeatedly generated.

Table 16–1 shows the calculation of the EMV value for IBM over a 67-day period in 1982. The additional columns show the 3-, 5-, 8-, 10-, and

Table 16–1
IBM: EASE OF MOVEMENT VALUES IN A 67-DAY PERIOD (1982)

Day	Box ratio	Midpoint move	Ease of movement	3-Day ease of movement	5-Day ease of movement	8-Day ease of movement	10-Day ease of movement	13-Day ease of movement
1	1.00							
2	.80	+ 1.50	+ 1.88					
3	.83	+ 2.00	+ 2.41					
4	1.50	+ 1.50	+ 1.00	+ 5.29				
5	1.00	–0–	–0–	+ 3.41				
6	1.50	+ 1.50	+ 1.00	+ 2.00	+ 6.29			
7	1.50	+ .50	+ .33	+ 1.33	+ 4.74			
8	1.00	+ 1.00	+ 1.00	+ 2.33	+ 3.33			
9	1.00	–0–	–0–	+ 1.33	+ 2.33	+ 7.62		
10	.55	+ 1.50	+ 2.73	+ 3.73	+ 5.06	+ 8.47		
11	1.50	+ 5.00	+ 3.33	+ 6.06	+ 7.39	+ 9.39	+13.68	
12	1.33	+ 2.50	+ 1.89	+ 7.95	+ 8.95	+10.28	+13.69	
13	.20	– .50	– 2.50	+ 2.72	+ 5.45	+ 7.78	+ 8.78	
14	1.67	– 4.00	– 2.40	– 3.01	+ 3.05	+ 4.38	+ 5.38	+11.68
15	1.50	+ .50	+ .33	– 4.57	+ .65	+ 4.38	+ 5.71	+10.13
16	1.33	+ 3.50	+ 2.63	+ .56	– .05	+ 6.01	+ 7.34	+10.35
17	1.40	+ 3.00	+ 2.14	+ 5.10	+ .20	+ 8.15	+ 9.15	+11.49
18	1.25	+ 1.50	+ 1.20	+ 5.97	+ 3.90	+ 6.62	+ 9.35	+12.69
19	1.00	– 1.50	– 1.50	+ 1.84	+ 4.80	+ 1.79	+ 7.85	+10.19
20	1.33	– 1.00	– .75	– 1.05	+ 3.72	– .85	+ 4.37	+ 9.11
21	1.50	– 2.50	– 1.67	– 3.92	– .58	– .02	– .63	+ 6.44
22	1.33	+ .50	+ .38	– 2.04	– 2.34	+ 2.76	– 2.14	+ 6.82
23	.67	–0–	–0–	– 1.29	– 3.54	+ 2.43	+ .36	+ 4.09
24	1.00	+ 2.00	+ 2.00	+ 2.38	– .04	+ 1.80	+ 4.76	+ 2.76
25	2.50	+ .50	+ .20	+ 2.20	+ .91	– .14	+ 4.63	+ 1.07
26	4.00	– .50	– .13	+ 2.07	+ 2.45	– 1.47	– 1.87	+ 3.44
27	3.00	–0–	–0–	+ .07	+ 2.07	+ .03	– .27	+ 5.84
28	1.00	– 1.50	– 1.50	– 1.63	+ .57	– .72	– 2.97	+ 4.01
29	.40	+ 1.00	+ 2.50	+ 1.00	+ 1.07	+ 3.45	+ 1.03	+ 3.88
30	.75	– 2.50	– 3.33	– 2.33	– 2.46	– .26	– 1.55	– 1.59
31	1.00	– .50	– .50	– 1.33	– 2.83	– .76	– .38	– 3.17
32	.33	– .50	– 1.52	– 5.35	– 4.35	– 4.28	– 2.28	– 3.19
33	1.00	– 2.00	– 2.00	– 4.02	– 4.85	– 6.48	– 4.28	– 4.44
34	1.50	– 1.00	– .67	– 4.19	– 8.02	– 7.02	– 6.95	– 3.44
35	.75	– 1.00	– 1.33	– 4.00	– 6.02	– 8.35	– 8.48	– 5.15
36	.75	– 1.00	– 1.33	– 3.33	– 6.85	– 8.18	– 9.68	– 6.48
37	2.50	+ .50	+ .20	– 2.46	– 5.13	–10.48	– 9.48	– 8.28
38	1.50	1.50	– 1.00	– 2.13	– 4.13	– 8.15	– 8.98	– 9.48
39	1.00	–0–	–0–	– .80	– 3.46	– 7.65	–11.48	– 9.35
40	1.00	– 1.00	– 1.00	– 2.00	– 3.13	– 7.13	– 9.15	–10.35
41	.75	+ 1.00	+ 1.33	+ .33	– .47	– 3.80	– 7.32	– 7.52
42	1.00	– 2.50	– 2.50	– 2.17	– 3.17	– 5.63	– 8.30	–12.52
43	1.50	–0–	–0–	– 1.17	– 2.17	– 4.30	– 6.30	– 9.19
44	2.00	+ .50	+ .25	– 2.25	– 1.92	– 2.72	– 5.38	– 8.44
45	1.00	– .50	– .50	– .25	– 1.42	– 3.42	– 4.55	– 7.42

Table 16–1 *(concluded)*

Day	Box ratio	Midpoint move	Ease of movement	3-Day ease of movement	5-Day ease of movement	8-Day ease of movement	10-Day ease of movement	13-Day ease of movement
46	.50	− 3.00	− 6.00	− 6.25	− 8.75	− 8.42	− 9.22	−11.42
47	1.25	− 3.50	− 2.80	− 9.30	− 9.05	−11.22	−12.22	−13.55
48	1.57	− 4.50	− 2.87	−11.67	−11.92	−13.09	−14.09	−15.09
49	1.50	− 3.50	− 2.33	− 8.00	−14.50	−16.75	−16.42	−16.09
50	1.00	+ 2.00	+ 2.00	− 3.20	−12.00	−12.25	−13.42	−14.29
51	1.50	+ 4.50	+ 3.00	+ 2.67	− 3.00	− 9.25	−11.75	−10.29
52	2.00	+ 1.50	+ .75	+ 5.75	+ .55	− 8.75	− 8.50	− 9.54
53	1.00	−0−	−0−	+ 3.75	+ 3.42	− 8.25	− 8.50	− 8.54
54	1.00	+ 1.50	+ 1.50	+ 2.25	+ 7.25	− .75	− 7.25	− 8.37
55	1.67	− 3.50	− 2.10	− .60	+ 3.15	− .05	− 8.85	− 7.97
56	2.00	− 1.50	− .75	− 1.35	− .60	+ 2.07	− 3.60	− 8.72
57	.80	+ 2.00	+ 2.50	− .35	+ 1.15	+ 6.90	+ 1.70	− 6.47
58	.50	+ 2.50	+ 5.00	+ 6.75	+ 6.15	+ 9.90	+ 9.57	− .97
59	.71	+ 4.00	+ 5.60	+13.10	+10.25	+12.50	+17.56	+10.63
60	1.33	+ 1.00	+ .75	+11.35	+13.10	+12.50	+16.31	+14.18
61	1.50	− 1.50	− 1.00	+ 5.35	+12.85	+11.50	+12.31	+16.05
62	.60	+ 1.50	+ 2.50	+ 2.25	+12.85	+12.50	+14.06	+20.88
63	.67	+ 1.00	+ 1.50	+ 3.00	+ 9.35	+16.10	+15.56	+23.58
64	1.33	−0−	−0−	+ 4.00	+ 3.75	+16.85	+14.06	+20.58
65	1.00	− 2.00	− 2.00	− .50	+ 1.00	+12.35	+14.16	+17.83
66	1.00	− 1.00	− 1.00	− 3.00	+ 1.00	+ 6.35	+14.35	+16.83
67	.40	− 1.00	− 2.50	− 5.50	− 4.00	− 1.75	+ 9.35	+12.83

13-day moving averages of the EMV, respectively. Figure 16–1 illustrates the price action of IBM on an Equivolume chart over the same period. Below the chart, we have plotted the three-day EMV values.

From the starting point of the chart until day 14, one would be long on the stock (or the options). Between 14 and 16 is a whipsaw, which could be costly. We have, however, seen that the stock has become indecisive after the advance and would be unlikely to follow the next buy (16) for this reason. The sell at 20 would reinforce the prior signal that the stock was having trouble advancing, and the weak buy at 23 would still not look very attractive. The sell at 27, while still in a trading range, would mean little except to confirm the indecision affecting the stock. By day 30, the sell seems to make

Figure 16–1
IBM—DAILY (interval: 200,000 shares; three-day ease of movement)

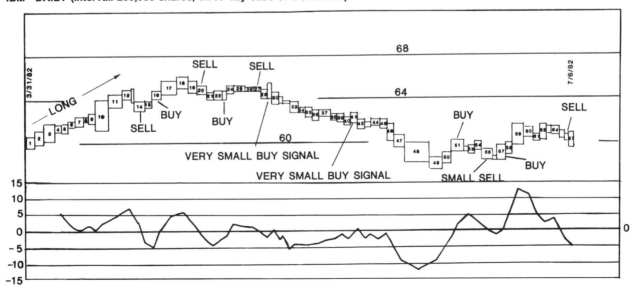

more sense. At day 41, the stock has been dropping well, and the slight move into plus territory seems to mean little. We would probably wait to see if the sell became stronger. It doesn't; the stock continues to drop through day 49, and then the rally to day 51 generates a buy signal. This looks more legitimate, and should be followed. Another whipsaw of small proportions at 55 to 57 might be ignored, due to the small numbers, but the final posting at 67 gives a strong enough sell signal to require action.

As can be seen from the above example, the three-day moving average gives many signals, some stronger than others. It does give worthwhile information very early in a move, but its volatility requires a good deal of judgment as to the strength or weakness of the signal and a cognizance of what has gone before. It is a worthwhile tool for the very aggressive short-term trader or options trader but much too volatile to be followed blindly as a strictly mathematical system. Judgment must play a large part in the decisions. Perhaps a longer-term approach would work better.

Figure 16–2 shows the same stock, over the same period, but now using a five-day moving average instead of a three-day. Here we have a somewhat less volatile indicator that gives fewer signals, has fewer whipsaws, comes in slightly later than the three-day, but is quite effective. The first sell of any consequence shows up on day 22, at a lower level than day 20 on the three-day chart. This is followed by a weak buy at 25 and another sell at day 30. If one followed every signal, one would have had two small losses in this topping area before participating in the very profitable move downward. At day 52, the signal to cover shorts and go long appears and stays in effect, ignoring the tiny dip at 56 until the sell signal at day 67.

Our conclusion: The five-day is better than the three-day, but still calls for judgmental decisions and is prone to whipsaws. It is primarily a speculator's tool, and requires immediate decisions. As with the three-day, it should not be used mechanically, but judgmentally.

If the five-day is better than the three-day, one would expect an eight-day to be even better. This is not true. The eight-day is an in-between value. It is too insensitive for the aggressive trader and too liable to whipsaws to be a good tool for less aggressive traders or investors. Figure 16–3 shows the results using this parameter. As with the five-day, the major moves are profitable, but the in and out points are later. The indecisive areas are still costly, however.

Figure 16–2
IBM—DAILY (interval: 200,000 shares; five-day ease of movement)

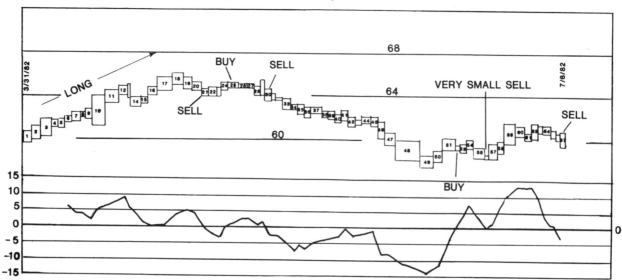

Figure 16–3
IBM—DAILY (interval: 200,000 shares; eight-day ease of movement)

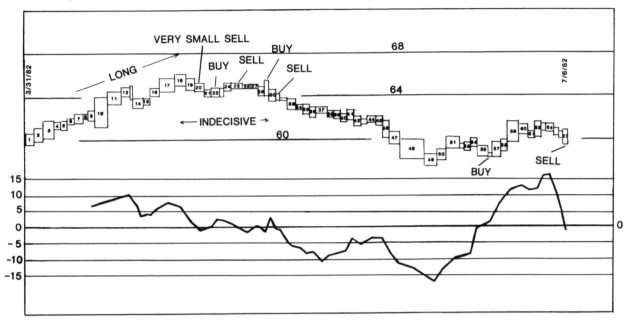

Perhaps because it is easy to calculate, a 10-day moving average has always been a favorite tool among technicians. We have experimented extensively with this and have found it to be of more value than the eight-day, but still not as effective as we would like. Figure 16–4 shows the results using a 10-day moving average.

The last chart (Figure 16–5) shows the results using a 13-day moving average of the EMV. Now we have reduced the sensitivity of the index enough to eliminate the whipsaw effect in the sideways areas, or the small pullbacks. It means that the signals come later, but are more likely to be correct. Later signals mean that the first part of a move is missed, and the stock has to

Figure 16–4
IBM—DAILY (interval: 200,000 shares; 10-day ease of movement)

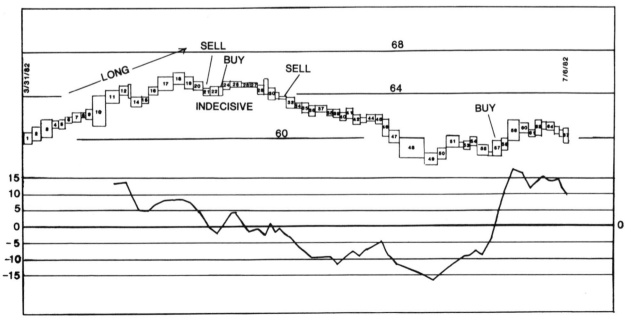

Figure 16–5
IBM—DAILY (interval: 200,000 shares; 13-day ease of movement)

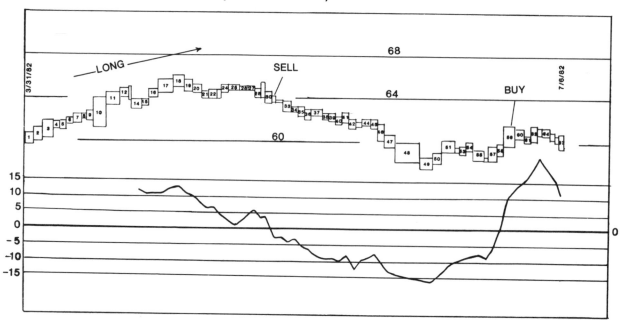

turn quite far back in the other direction before a close-out signal. Consequently, a part of the potential profit is lost. Experimentation with many values for the EMV has convinced us, however, that the 13-day value is the best we have worked with. It appears to be the lowest number that will avoid most whipsaws. Any larger number makes the signals later, thereby reducing profits, and provides no additional benefits.

Chapter 17   Ease of Movement on a Weekly Basis

To this point, we have been looking at daily charts and capitalizing on the fairly short-term fluctuations. For this purpose we have found that the 13-day moving average of the EMV is quite effective. This method is meant for traders, whose purpose is speculative and whose temperament allows very active market participation. Others may wish to be somewhat less aggressive, holding stock positions for a number of months and ignoring the smaller gyrations, while utilizing the larger moves. For this purpose, we suggest keeping weekly charts instead of daily charts, but still using the EMV calculations in accordance with the technique we will illustrate in this chapter.

There are two reasons for using weekly Equivolume charts. The first is mechanical. It would be possible to use daily charts, making the EMV less sensitive by calculating a longer-term moving average. It creates a very long chart, however, with which it is hard to work. It also means daily calculations, which quickly develop into an office stacked with past data. The weekly charts reduce the size of the charts and greatly simplify the calculations.

The second reason for using weekly charts and calculations is psychological. A longer-term investor who is, nevertheless, looking at daily numbers finds it difficult not to succumb to the emotional pressures that the daily gyrations elicit. In order to remain a systematic investor, he must avoid emotional involvement. Decisions should be made in a businesslike manner, without being influenced by the pressures of fear and greed. Weekly charts obscure the minor ripples and make the more important moves apparent. By posting charts and doing calculations on the weekend, an investor is better able to maintain his objectivity and not react to minor ripples.

The methodology remains the same when using weekly charts. The EMV is calculated in exactly the same manner except that the midpoint moves are, of course, week to week. Figure 17–1 covers the trading on K mart over a year and a half in 1981 and 1982. Accompanying these charts are the calculations of the EMV with moving averages, using 3-week, 5-week, 8-week, 10-week, and 13-week values (Table 17–1).

The first information that we look for after calculating these EMV moving averages is continuity. Signals that are close together and erratic are harmful. We do not want to be moving in and out of a stock again and again, since this costs commissions and is less likely to create profits.

Glancing down the listing of the three-week average, we see that there are a number of instances in which the numbers stay positive or negative for only a week or two. Obviously, this is too sensitive an indicator for our purposes. Comparing the buy and sell points to the chart, we see that most trades would have been unprofitable and a few would have been very costly. The five-week moving average has almost as many false signals as the three-

Figure 17–1
K MART—WEEKLY (interval: 200,000 shares)

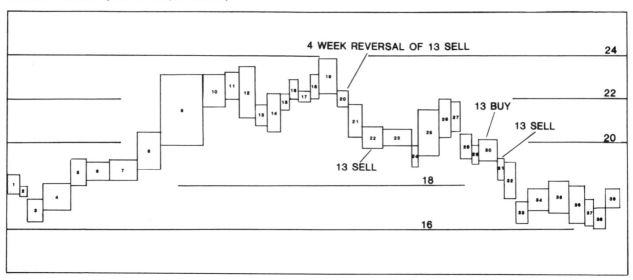

week and does little to help catch the major moves—again, too sensitive an indicator.

Looking down the list of values for the eight-week moving average of the EMV, we see much better continuity. Once it goes from positive to negative, it tends to stay there for a reasonable number of weeks. It generates a short sale on week 19, which leads to a quick profit by buying at the next signal at week 28. This buy, however, is costly, being closed out at week 33. A short position from week 33 to week 50 is a breakeven—but costs commissions. The next long position, from week 50 to week 67, is quite profitable. The eight-week moving average is obviously an improvement but still contains a number of whipsaws.

Since the 8-week was such an improvement over the lower divisors, one would expect the 10-week to be even better. That does not appear to be so. At the top, it gives a later and lower sell signal than does the 8-week and then swings wildly from plus to minus and back a number of profitless times in the base area. It catches the upmove starting at week 55, but gets out late at week 67. Evidently, the 10-week is not the answer either.

Looking now at the 13-week numbers, we see that there is fairly good continuity, but a few false signals are still generated. This happens at week

Figure 17–1 *(concluded)*

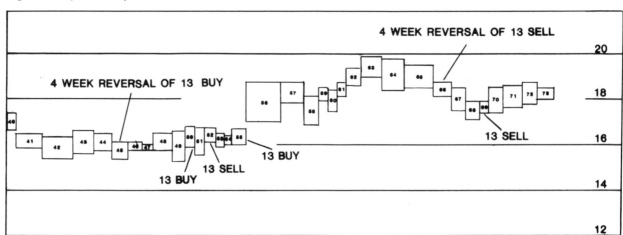

Table 17–1
K MART EMVs IN 1981 AND 1982

Week	Box ratio	Midpoint move	Ease of movement	3-Week ease of movement	5-Week ease of movement	8-Week ease of movement	10-Week ease of movement	13-Week ease of movement	
1	.71								
2	.75	− 2.5	− 3.33						
3	.88	− 7.0	− 7.95						
4	1.20	+ 5.0	+ 4.17	− 7.11					
5	.70	+ 9.0	+12.86	+ 9.08					
6	1.43	+ .5	+ .33	+17.36	+ 6.08				
7	1.50	+ .5	+ .33	+13.52	+ 9.74				
8	.77	+ 7.0	+ 9.09	+ 9.75	+26.78				
9	.73	+15.0	+20.55	+29.97	+43.16	+36.05			
10	.83	+ 7.0	+ 8.43	+38.07	+38.73	+47.81			
11	.60	+ 2.0	+ 3.33	+32.31	+41.73	+59.09	+47.81		
12	.37	− 2.5	− 6.76	+ 5.00	+34.64	+48.16	+44.38		
13	.63	− 8.5	−13.49	−16.92	+12.06	+21.81	+38.84		
14	.43	+ 1.0	+ 2.33	−17.92	− 6.16	+23.81	+37.00	+29.89	
15	.67	+ 4.0	+ 5.97	+ 5.19	− 8.62	+29.45	+30.11	+39.19	Up
16	.57	+ 4.5	+ 7.89	+16.19	− 4.06	+28.25	+37.67	+55.03	Up
17	1.25	− 2.5	− 2.00	+11.86	+ .70	+ 5.70	+35.34	+48.86	Down
18	.44	+ 3.5	+ 7.95	+13.84	+22.14	+ 5.22	+34.20	+43.95	Down
19	.62	− 4.0	− 6.45	− .50	+13.35	− 4.56	+ 7.20	+37.17	Down
20	.83	− 8.5	−10.24	− 8.74	− 2.86	− 8.04	−11.47	+26.60	Down*
21	.50	− 8.0	−16.00	−32.69	−26.75	−10.55	−30.80	+ 1.51	Down
22	1.13	− 6.0	− 5.31	+31.55	−30.06	−18.19	−29.35	−24.35	Down
23	2.00	–0–	–0–	−21.31	−38.01	−24.16	−15.86	−32.78	Down
24	.38	− 7.0	−18.42	−23.73	−49.98	−50.47	−36.61	−54.53	Down†
25	.53	+ 8.5	+16.04	− 2.38	−23.70	−32.43	−26.54	−31.73	Up
26	.36	+ 5.5	+15.78	+13.40	+ 8.08	−24.60	−18.65	− 2.46	Up
27	.36	+ .5	+ 1.39	+33.21	+14.78	−16.76	−15.26	− 3.40	Down
28	.56	+11.0	+22.00	+39.17	+36.78	+15.48	− 1.21	−12.63	Down
29	.43	− 3.0	− 6.98	+16.41	+48.22	+24.50	− 1.74	− 2.24	Up
30	1.00	+ 1.5	+ 1.50	+16.52	+33.68	+31.31	+10.60	+ 1.26	Up
31	.33	− 7.0	−21.21	−26.69	− 3.31	+10.10	+ 5.39	−27.90	Down
32	.36	− 4.0	−11.11	−30.82	−15.81	+17.41	− 1.01	−32.56	Down
33	.63	−12.0	−19.08	−51.40	−56.88	−17.71	−20.09	−41.40	Down
34	1.13	+ 5.0	+ 4.42	−25.77	−45.48	−29.07	+ 2.75	−20.98	Up
35	.75	+ 1.0	+ 1.33	−13.33	−45.65	−29.13	− 3.96	−14.34	Up
36	.50	− 3.0	− 6.00	− .25	−30.44	−57.13	−33.74	−20.34	Down
37	.30	− 3.0	−10.00	−14.67	−29.33	−60.15	−45.13	−11.92	Up
38	.63	− 2.0	− 3.17	−19.17	−13.42	−64.82	−70.30	−31.13	Down
39	1.00	+ 8.0	+ 8.00	− 5.17	− 9.84	−35.61	−55.32	−39.11	Down
40	1.00	− 4.0	− 4.00	− .83	−15.17	−28.50	−60.82	−44.50	Down
41	2.20	− 6.5	− 2.95	+ 1.05	−12.12	−12.37	−42.56	−69.45	Down*
42	1.63	− 2.5	− 1.53	− 8.48	− 3.65	−18.32	−32.98	−64.00	Up
43	1.13	+ 2.0	+ 1.77	− 2.71	+ 1.29	−17.88	−12.13	−63.73	Up
44	1.33	–0–	–0–	+ .24	− 6.71	−11.88	−16.55	−42.52	Up
45	1.17	− 3.0	− 2.56	− .79	− 5.27	− 4.44	−20.44	−33.97	Up†
46	2.00	+ 1.5	+ .75	− 1.81	− 1.57	− .52	−13.69	−14.14	Up
47	2.50	− .5	− .20	− 2.01	− .24	− 8.72	− 3.89	−18.56	Down
48	1.14	+ 2.0	+ 1.75	+ 2.30	− .26	− 2.97	+ 1.03	−18.14	Up
49	.55	− 1.5	− 2.73	− 1.18	− 2.99	− 2.75	− 9.70	−14.87	Up
50	.50	+ 2.5	+ 5.00	+ 4.02	+ 4.57	+ 3.78	− .70	+ .13	Up
51	.40	− 1.0	− 2.50	− .23	+ 1.32	− .49	− .25	+ .80	Up†
52	1.00	+ 2.5	+ 2.50	+ 5.00	+ 4.02	+ 2.01	+ 3.78	− 4.70	Down
53	.80	− 2.0	− 2.50	− 2.50	− .23	+ 2.07	− .49	− 3.20	Up
54	1.00	–0–	–0–	–0–	+ 2.50	+ 1.32	− .49	− .25	Up
55	1.00	+ 1.5	+ 1.50	− 1.00	− 1.00	+ 3.02	+ 3.57	+ 2.78	Up
56	1.07	+12.0	+11.21	+12.71	+12.71	+12.48	+14.03	+13.22	Up†
57	1.58	+ 3.5	+ 2.22	+14.93	+12.43	+17.43	+16.45	+14.44	Up
58	.70	− 6.5	− 9.28	+ 4.15	+ 5.65	+ 3.15	+ 5.42	+ 7.72	Down
59	.80	+ 5.5	+ 6.88	− .18	+12.53	+12.53	+15.03	+13.85	Up
60	.50	− 2.5	− 5.00	− 7.40	+ 6.03	+ 5.03	+ 5.03	+ 9.05	Down
61	.80	+ 4.5	+ 5.63	+ 7.51	+ .45	+13.16	+13.16	+12.93	Up

Table 17–1 *(concluded)*

Week	Box ratio	Midpoint move	Ease of movement	3-Week ease of movement	5-Week ease of movement	8-Week ease of movement	10-Week ease of movement	13-Week ease of movement	
62	1.00	+ 4.5	+ 4.50	+ 5.31	+ 2.73	+17.66	+15.16	+20.16	Up
63	1.29	+ 3.0	+ 2.33	+12.46	+14.34	+18.49	+19.99	+17.49	Down
64	.82	− 2.5	− 3.05	+ 3.78	+ 4.41	+ 4.23	+16.94	+16.94	Down
65	1.50	− .5	− .33	− 1.05	+ 9.08	+ 1.68	+15.11	+14.11	Down
66	1.60	− 4.5	− 2.81	− 6.19	+ .64	+ 8.15	+ 1.10	+13.80	Down*
67	.75	− 3.5	− 4.67	− 7.81	− 8.53	− 3.40	− 5.80	+ 9.13	Down
68	1.00	− 4.0	− 4.00	−11.48	−14.86	− 2.40	− .52	+ 3.63	Down
69	1.00	+ 1.0	+ 1.00	− 7.67	−10.81	− 7.03	− 6.40	−15.25	Down
70	.67	+ 2.5	+ 3.73	+ .73	+ 4.06	− 7.80	+ 2.33	−16.74	Down
71	1.00	+ 1.5	+ 1.50	+ 6.23	+ 8.37	−11.63	− 1.80	− 1.23	Up
72	.88	+ 1.0	+ 1.14	+ 6.37	+14.18	− 7.44	− 5.16	− 1.74	Down
73	1.75	−0−	−0−	+ 2.64	+18.18	− 7.11	− 7.49	+ 5.90	Up

* Four consecutive downs—the signal to sell.
† Four consecutive ups—the signal that the stock has reversed to the upside.

30 and again at week 50. It helps in recognizing the profitable major moves, but tends to be a bit late. We have shown on the chart the points where the 13-week numbers go from plus to minus and minus to plus, labeling them "13 (buy)" and "13 (sell)." We can see that the sell on week 22 misses much of the profit due to its tardiness. A similar thing happens at week 69. It would seem that the 13-week, unlike the 13-day on our daily charts, has many weaknesses.

We have found, however, that the continuity of the 13-week average does provide us with some answers. It accurately recognizes the major moves, but does so somewhat late. Looking back at the column of numbers that constitute the 13-week moving average, perhaps we can see a better way to use them.

These numbers tend to go to peaks that coincide with or often are slightly before the stock makes its highs. Conversely, they tend to go to the greatest minus values at or slightly before the stock makes its lows. In waiting for the values to cross over from plus to minus or minus to plus, we tend to be late. If, instead, we try to recognize the points where the maximums and minimums occur we will be somewhat earlier. We have found that a satisfactory solution is arrived at by waiting until the 13-week moving average of the EMV has changed direction and progressed in that direction for four consecutive weeks, and then acting. This allows for smaller resting areas which do not reverse the stock's direction on a longer-term basis, yet recognizes most major moves early enough to produce profitable positions. The table for K mart shows how this has been done. Each week's entry is followed by an entry of "Up" or "Down." This entry is merely the comparison of that week to the prior week. The first such notation is week 15 and is shown as up because the value for week 15, +39.19, was higher than the prior week's value of +29.89.

Week 17 is shown as down because its value, +48.86, is lower than the prior week's value of +55.03. Assuming that we were long the stock from the prior signal, we are now watching for a string of four consecutive down notations, which will be our signal to sell. This occurs on week 20, since weeks 17, 18, 19, and 20 all bear down notations. We have marked that week with an asterisk.

Since we are short (or out of the stock) on week 20, we will now be watching for four up notations in a row to tell us that the stock has again reversed to the upside. That signal, also marked by an asterisk, is seen at week 45, telling us it is time to cover shorts and go long.

The next signal is four downs at week 66. (The four ups at week 57 is only a confirming signal, since we have already bought.) This signal is still in effect at the end of our data.

The signals are marked in Figure 17–1 as "four-week reversal of 13 (buy)" and "four-week reversal of 13 (sell)." As can be seen, all of the whipsaws were avoided, and the signals were better than those developed by just using the crossovers of the 13-week EMV from plus to minus or minus to plus. One stock does not prove the case, however. We must look at a number of companies in various industries to see if the method is reliable.

Let us consider the 13-week EMV figures for Ford, shown in Table 17–2 and relate them to the chart of Ford (Figure 17–2). Although we do not

Table 17–2
FORD EMVs

Week	Ease of movement	13-Week ease of movement	
2	+ 7.00		
3	− 3.33		
4	− 6.82		
5	− 2.50		
6	− 7.46		
7	− 1.67		
8	− 1.20		
9	− 1.25		
10	− 7.04		
11	−12.50		
12	+ 8.00		
13	−31.48		
14	−18.42	− 78.67	
15	−11.40	− 97.07	Down
16	− 4.48	− 98.22	Down
17	− 9.70	−101.10	Down
18	+12.00	− 86.60	Up
19	+ 6.94	− 72.20	Up
20	+ 4.00	− 66.53	Up
21	− .60	− 65.93	Up*
22	− 5.00	− 69.68	Down
23	+ 1.67	− 60.97	Up
24	+ 1.25	− 47.22	Up
25	+ 1.88	− 53.34	Down
26	+ 7.50	− 14.36	Up
27	+11.67	+ 15.73	Up
28	+ 3.64	+ 30.77	Up
29	− 4.84	+ 20.41	Down
30	+ 5.97	+ 46.08	Up
31	−0−	+ 34.08	Down
32	+ .63	+ 27.77	Down
33	− .25	+ 23.52	Down
34	+19.35	+ 43.47	Up
35	+ 3.51	+ 51.98	Up
36	− .88	+ 49.43	Down
37	− 8.00	+ 40.18	Down
38	−10.45	+ 27.85	Down
39	+ 5.33	+ 25.68	Down†
40	− 8.77	+ 5.24	Down
41	− 9.65	− 8.05	Down
42	− 8.00	− 11.21	Down
43	− 1.32	− 18.50	Down
44	− 5.00	− 23.50	Down
45	− 4.07	− 28.20	Down
46	− 3.33	− 31.28	Down
47	− 5.33	− 55.96	Down

Table 17-2 *(concluded)*

Week	Ease of movement	13-Week ease of movement	
48	− 5.98	− 65.45	Down
49	− 2.99	− 67.56	Down
50	+ 2.08	− 57.48	Up
51	+ 1.88	− 45.15	Up
52	+ 8.35	− 42.13	Up
53	− 2.26	− 35.62	Up*
54	− 1.75	− 27.72	Up
55	− 4.65	− 24.37	Up
56	+ 1.67	− 21.38	Up
57	+ 5.81	− 10.57	Up
58	− 6.00	− 12.50	Up
59	−0−	− 9.17	Up

* Four consecutive ups—the signal that the stock has reversed to the upside.
† Four consecutive downs—the signal to sell.

show the earlier numbers, the long decline prior to week 14 implies that our last signal would have been a sell signal, and we would, at the beginning of our data, be looking for a string of four consecutive buys in order to go to the long side. This signal comes in at week 21. Note that this signal is six weeks before the 13-week figures actually go to the plus side, and at a much more advantageous price level. The lowest number we saw during the decline was −101.10, on week 17. Ideally, of course, that would have been the time to buy, but we had to wait until week 21 to have our four-week reversal signal.

The next signal, a series of four sells, is seen at week 39, representing a substantial gain and indicating it is time to take profits and perhaps go short. The highest reading we had for the EMV-13 was +51.98, on week 35, but we could not know that until later. The stock does drop sharply from week 39, and the indicator keeps us from buying or covering short positions until week 53, when four ups again say to buy the stock. Again, the lowest reading was made before our signal, at week 49. It would have been nice to cover on that week, but only future trading told us that. This method assumes that we will usually not buy on the exact bottom or sell on the exact top,

Figure 17-2
FORD—WEEKLY (interval: 200,000 shares)

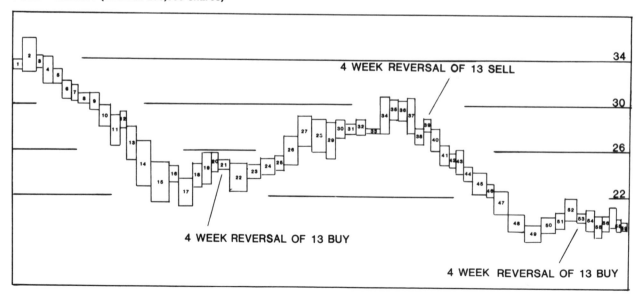

but relies on the assumption that our signals will come in early enough so that the move will still have further to go, allowing us a piece out of the middle.

Figure 17–3 and its accompanying Table 17–3 show the results using National Distillers over a 2½ year period ending in April 1982. During this period, the stock went through a number of substantial up and down moves. As the numbers show, the 13-week crossovers would have produced a number of costly signals. Utilizing the four-week reversal of the 13 method, however, we reduce this to only four signals, two buys and two sells, all of which produce profits. As we have noted in other examples, the signals do not catch the absolute tops and bottoms in most cases. This is unnecessary if we can make only a few trades over this fairly long period, and yet participate correctly in the major moves. The desire to sell at the exact top can be dangerous since it injects a greed factor. A business-like approach to the market requires that we act in accordance with an established system. Tops are only recognizable in retrospect. We only want to identify them soon enough so that we do not give back all our profits.

Some stocks work better than others utilizing this method. A stock like National Distillers has fairly regular ups and downs and contains few surprises. An established trend continues for a long time, without many dramatic reversals. The chart shows a smoothness and a reliability. Such a stock is ideal in our EMV analyses. Other stocks may, due perhaps to thin capitalization, high speculative interest, volatility of their industry, erratic earnings, or lack of dividends, produce much less reliable charts. They tend to show great variety in volume and sudden violent price moves. Such stocks can, if used correctly, produce much larger profits and do it more rapidly, but they carry, likewise, an increased risk. Tops and bottoms tend to be sharper, making our signals late and erasing a larger part of our profits. Such stocks can be used, but the investor should be aware of the increased risk.

Figure 17–4 and Table 17–4 of this chapter show a stock, Northwest Airlines, with such a price history. Note the rapid moves on weeks 12, 30, and 50. In each case, an orderly decline of many weeks has been erased in one week of trading. The reversal signal comes in later, after the move has progressed quite far. It should be noted that each signal was followed by a continuation of the move, and the investor would have been in a profit position, but the next volatile move tended to erase much of that profit.

All of these stocks we have worked with in this section have essentially gone nowhere over the period studied. As we have seen, even though there has been no real progress, they have all been able to produce profits for

Figure 17–3
NATIONAL DISTILLERS—WEEKLY (interval: 100,000 shares)

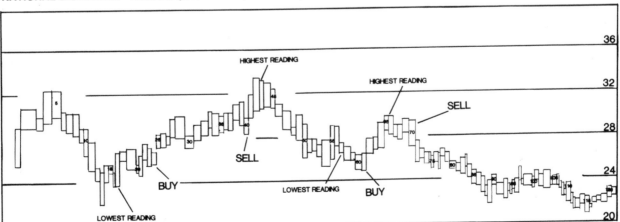

Figure 17–4
NORTHWEST AIRLINES—WEEKLY (interval: 100,000 shares)

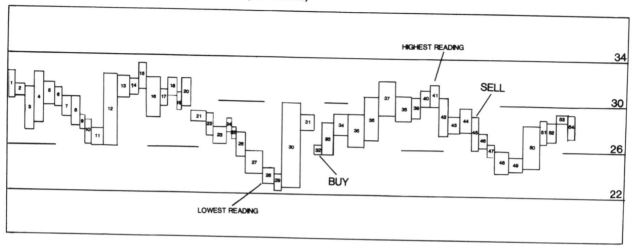

Table 17–3
NATIONAL DISTILLERS EMVs

Week	Ease of movement	13-Week ease of movement	
2	+10.50		
3	− 2.67		
4	+19.70		
5	+ 2.50		
6	−19.70		
7	− 2.00		
8	− 1.62		
9	− 8.75		
10	−12.50		
11	−16.67		
12	−14.00		
13	−29.41		
14	+ 1.52	− 73.10	
15	+ 2.24	− 81.36	Down
16	−20.00	− 98.69	Down
17	+17.68	−100.71	Down
18	+ 5.50	− 97.71	Up
19	− 1.75	− 79.76	Up
20	−10.61	− 88.37	Down
21	+ 3.45	− 81.30	Up
22	+15.00	− 57.55	Up
23	− 6.06	− 51.11	Up
24	− 1.00	− 35.44	Up*
25	+16.25	− 5.19	Up
26	+ 1.25	+ 25.47	Up
27	− .75	+ 23.20	Down
28	+13.64	+ 34.60	Up
29	+ 1.00	+ 55.60	Up
30	− 5.50	+ 32.42	Down
31	+ 5.00	+ 31.92	Down
32	+ 3.33	+ 35.00	Up
33	+ 9.00	+ 54.61	Up
34	+ 3.95	+ 55.11	Down
35	−0−	+ 40.11	Up
36	+ 3.00	+ 49.17	Down
37	− 1.52	+ 48.65	Down
38	+ 5.83	+ 38.23	Down
39	− 2.27	+ 34.71	Down†
40	−13.64	+ 21.82	Up

Table 17–3 *(continued)*

Week	Ease of movement	13-Week ease of movement	
41	+28.00	+ 36.18	Up
42	+14.00	+ 49.18	Up
43	+ 2.27	+ 56.95	Down
44	–0–	+ 51.95	Down
45	− 3.45	+ 54.17	Down
46	− 6.00	+ 30.17	Down†
47	− 6.14	+ 20.08	Down
48	− 5.97	+ 14.11	Down
49	+ 3.00	+ 14.11	Unchanged
50	−29.41	− 13.78	Down
51	− 3.75	− 23.36	Down
52	–0–	− 21.09	Up
53	− 4.00	− 11.45	Up
54	− 2.27	− 41.72	Down
55	+23.53	− 32.19	Up
56	+ 8.62	− 25.84	Up
57	− 6.72	− 32.56	Down
58	− 3.33	− 32.44	Up
59	− 1.49	− 27.93	Up
60	− 4.17	− 25.96	Up
61	–0–	− 19.99	Up*
62	+10.00	− 12.99	Up
63	+ 2.00	+ 18.42	Up
64	+ 9.00	+ 31.17	Up
65	+11.25	+ 42.42	Up
66	− 3.00	+ 43.42	Up
67	− 4.00	+ 41.69	Down
68	− 1.25	+ 16.91	Down
69	+ 4.17	+ 12.46	Down
70	− 9.00	+ 10.18	Down†
71	−26.00	− 12.49	Down
72	− 1.49	− 12.49	Unchanged
73	− 3.00	− 11.32	Up
74	–0–	− 11.32	Unchanged
75	− 6.00	− 27.32	Down
76	+ 2.24	− 27.08	Up
77	− 5.88	− 41.96	Down
78	+ 2.99	− 50.22	Down
79	− 2.99	− 50.21	Up
80	− 2.00	− 48.21	Up
81	− .74	− 47.71	Up
82	+ 1.52	− 50.35	Down
83	+ 6.00	− 35.35	Up
84	− 7.00	− 16.35	Up
85	− 5.00	− 19.86	Down
86	− 2.00	− 18.86	Up
87	− 5.00	− 23.86	Down
88	− 7.58	− 25.44	Down
89	–0–	− 27.68	Down
90	+12.12	− 9.68	Up
91	− 2.00	− 14.67	Down
92	–0–	− 11.68	Up
93	+ 1.52	− 8.16	Up
94	− 3.00	− 10.42	Down
95	+ 5.00	− 6.94	Up
96	+ 1.25	− 11.69	Down
97	+22.50	+ 17.81	Up
98	− 6.00	+ 6.81	Down
99	+ .50	+ 19.31	Up
100	− 3.00	+ 21.31	Up
101	+ 3.73	+ 32.62	Up
102	− 4.00	+ 28.62	Down

Table 17–3 *(concluded)*

Week	Ease of movement	13-Week ease of movement	
103	+ 1.00	+ 17.50	Down
104	− 2.00	+ 17.50	Unchanged
105	+ .75	+ 18.25	Up
106	+ 2.00	+ 18.73	Up
107	−10.00	+ 11.73	Down
108	− 6.00	+ .73	Down
109	+ 5.00	+ 4.48	Up
110	− 3.45	− 21.47	Down
111	− 4.00	− 19.47	Down
112	− 8.00	− 27.97	Down
113	− .75	− 25.72	Up
114	+ 2.24	− 27.21	Down
115	− 4.55	− 27.76	Down
116	−0−	− 28.76	Down
117	+ 1.50	− 25.26	Up
118	+ .50	− 25.51	Down
119	−0−	− 27.51	Down
120	+ 5.00	− 12.51	Up
121	−0−	− 6.51	Up

* Four consecutive ups—the signal that the stock has reversed to the upside.
† Four consecutive downs—the signal to sell.

Table 17–4
NORTHWEST AIRLINES EMVs

Week	Ease of movement	13-Week ease of movement	
2	− 2.00		
3	−24.07		
4	+14.58		
5	+ 7.53		
6	− 3.00		
7	− 5.26		
8	− 3.75		
9	−10.00		
10	− 9.21		
11	− 1.81		
12	+39.58		
13	+11.27		
14	−0−	+13.86	
15	+13.64	+29.50	Up
16	−17.44	+36.13	Up
17	−0−	+21.55	Down
18	+ 5.22	+19.24	Down
19	−15.15	+ 7.09	Down
20	+ 8.75	+21.20	Up
21	− 3.65	+21.30	Unchanged
22	− 6.58	+24.72	Up
23	− 4.00	+29.93	Up
24	+ 7.00	+38.74	Up
25	− 5.00	− 5.84	Down
26	− 7.02	−24.13	Down
27	− 6.00	−30.13	Down
28	− 5.00	−48.77	Down†
29	− 4.00	−35.33	Up
30	+41.07	+ 5.74	Up
31	+10.56	+11.08	Up
32	− 9.50	+16.73	Up*
33	+ 8.89	+16.87	Up
34	+ 5.00	+25.42	Up

Table 17-4 *(concluded)*

Week	Ease of movement	13-Week ease of movement	
35	− 3.13	+28.87	Up
36	+11.25	+44.12	Up
37	+12.07	+49.19	Up
38	− 4.49	+49.70	Up
39	−0−	+56.72	Up
40	+ 4.38	+67.10	Up
41	+ 1.75	+73.85	Up
42	−24.19	+53.66	Down
43	− 2.08	+10.51	Down
44	+ 2.38	+ 2.33	Down
45	−18.00	− 9.63	Down†
46	− 3.13	−18.19	Down
47	− 4.67	−27.15	Down
48	− 5.33	−30.06	Down
49	− .50	−41.81	Down
50	+12.77	−41.11	Up
51	+13.16	−23.46	Up
52	−0−	−23.46	Unchanged
53	+ 2.99	−24.85	Down
54	− 7.89	−34.49	Down

* Four consecutive ups—the signal that the stock has reversed to the upside.
† Four consecutive downs—the signal to sell.

both bulls and bears. An investor who had merely held the stocks throughout the period would have accomplished little except collect dividends, but a careful participant, following this method, would have made additional money through capital gains.

In the final sections of this book, we will look at methods whereby we can combine EMV work with cycles and trends, thereby enhancing our results by using stocks that are going somewhere rather than stocks that are going nowhere.

Chapter 18   Normalized Ease of Movement

To this point we have discussed EMV work, using visual rather than mathematical observations, working directly from our Equivolume charts and making calculations on a small calculator. We have found that our results are very good, treating every stock individually. There are two drawbacks. First, there is a lot of work to be done on each stock. It is a tedious process to calculate EMV moving averages each day or each week, and still watch a fairly large number of stocks. Second, the EMV values are somewhat a function of the scales we are using. A lower volume increment in the original chart leads to more square entries and, therefore, higher box ratios. Then, when we divide the midpoint move by the box ratio, we emerge with a lower EMV. If, on the other hand, we squeeze the chart vertically by using a less sensitive price scale, we again change the EMV values. The boxes, as before, become more square and the EMV values are therefore lowered.

These are not problems if we are looking at only one stock. Regardless of the scales used, the EMV values will go from plus to minus on the same day. Similarly, the changes up or down will only be affected in magnitude, not in direction. The problem arises when we try to compare one stock to another. The numerical magnitude of the EMV is meaningless when we compare it to another stock with different volume and range characteristics.

Ideally, we would like to be able to compare EMV values from one stock to another and thereby determine which stocks are more attractive. This calls for the calculation of a normalized EMV. In this chapter we will demonstrate the method of calculating a normalized EMV. It is a process which should be followed and understood in order to use normalized EMV values effectively. On the other hand, it is a very complicated and tedious procedure to do by hand, and is ideally suited to computer applications.

Normalization of the EMV requires that we look at all stocks in a similar manner, regardless of their volume and range characteristics. However, we do *not* want to normalize the price movement in such a way that volatile price action is hidden from our view. Volatility can work in our favor if our interpretation is correct. Our objective is to capitalize on the largest possible price move in the minimum time. A slow-moving stock may make us a profit, but a fast-moving stock could make us a profit much more rapidly.

Table 18–1 shows the results of calculating the EMV on a normalized basis.

Column 1—We have numbered each day of information. These numbers correspond to the numbered boxes on the accompanying chart (Figure 18–1).

Column 2—The high for the stock on that day.

Column 3—The low for the stock on that day.

Table 18–1
AETNA EMVs ON A NORMALIZED BASIS

1 Entry	2 Hi	3 Low	4 Volume	5 Range	6 Midpoint	7 Midpoint move	8 % Midpoint move	9 10-Day average volume	10 10-Day percent volume	11 10-Day average range	12 10-Day percent range	13 Box ratio	14 EMV
1	33½	32⅞	1,771	.625	33.1875								
2	33¾	33⅛	1,817	.625	33.4375	+ .250	+ .75						
3	34½	33½	1,400	1.000	34.000	+ .5625	+1.65						
4	34¼	33¾	946	.500	34.000	–0–	–0–						
5	34	33⅝	981	.375	33.8125	– .1875	– .55						
6	34¼	33⅝	1,302	.625	33.9375	+ .125	+ .37						
7	34½	34	4,179	.500	34.250	+ .3125	+ .91						
8	35½	34⅞	2,062	.625	35.1875	+ .9375	+2.66						
9	35½	34⅝	804	.875	35.0625	– .125	– .36						
10	34⅞	34⅜	1,610	.500	34.625	– .4375	–1.26	1,687	95	.625	80	1.19	–1.06
11	34½	33½	1,079	1.000	34.000	– .625	–1.84	1,618	67	.663	151	.44	–4.18
12	34	33⅜	2,387	.625	33.6875	– .3125	– .93	1,675	143	.663	94	1.52	– .61
13	33¾	33	1,961	.750	33.875	+ .1875	+ .55	1,731	113	.638	113	1.00	+ .55
14	34⅝	33¾	1,981	.875	34.1875	+ .3125	+ .91	1,835	108	.675	130	.83	+1.10
15	34⅝	34	1,641	.625	34.3125	+ .125	+ .36	1,901	86	.700	89	.97	+ .37
16	34½	34⅛	3,519	.375	34.3125	–0–	–0–	2,122	166	.675	56	2.96	–0–
17	34½	33¾	1,871	.750	34.125	– .1875	– .55	1,892	99	.700	107	.93	– .59
18	34⅛	33¾	1,985	.375	33.9375	– .1875	– .55	1,884	105	.675	56	1.88	– .29
19	34	33⅜	1,950	.625	33.6875	– .250	– .74	1,998	98	.650	96	1.02	– .73
20	33⅞	33½	2,455	.375	33.6875	–0–	–0–	2,083	118	.638	59	2.00	–0–
21	34	33¾	2,389	.250	33.875	+ .1875	+ .55	2,214	108	.563	44	2.45	+ .22
22	34⅞	34	3,396	.875	34.4375	+ .5625	+1.63	2,315	147	.588	149	.99	+1.65
23	36	34⅝	2,238	1.375	35.3125	+ .875	+2.48	2,343	96	.650	212	.45	+5.51
24	35¾	34¾	2,546	1.000	35.250	– .0625	– .18	2,399	106	.663	151	.70	– .26
25	34⅞	34½	349	.375	34.6875	– .5625	–1.62	2,270	15	.638	59	.25	–6.48
26	34½	34	1,488	.500	34.250	– .4375	–1.28	2,067	72	.650	77	.94	–1.36
27	34⅛	33⅜	2,060	.750	33.750	– .500	–1.48	2,086	99	.650	115	.86	–1.72
28	34⅛	33⅞	2,694	.250	34.000	+ .250	+ .74	2,157	125	.638	39	3.21	+ .23
29	34¼	33⅞	1,618	.375	34.0625	+ .0625	+ .18	2,123	76	.613	61	1.25	+ .14
30	34⅝	34⅛	1,749	.500	34.375	+ .3125	+ .91	2,053	85	.625	80	1.06	+ .86
31	35	34½	1,502	.500	34.750	+ .375	+1.08	1,964	76	.650	77	.99	+1.09
32	34⅝	34⅛	1,841	.500	34.375	– .375	–1.09	1,809	102	.613	82	1.24	– .88
33	34¼	33⅞	1,185	.375	34.0625	– .3125	– .92	1,703	70	.513	73	.96	– .96
34	34½	34⅛	1,850	.375	34.3125	+ .250	+ .73	1,634	113	.450	83	1.36	+ .54
35	34⅛	33⅝	1,065	.500	33.875	– .4375	–1.29	1,705	62	.463	108	.57	–2.26
36	33¾	33½	747	.250	33.625	– .250	– .74	1,631	46	.438	57	.81	– .91
37	33½	33¼	1,151	.250	33.375	– .250	– .75	1,540	75	.388	64	1.17	– .64
38	33⅝	33⅛	2,674	.500	33.375	–0–	–0–	1,538	174	.413	121	1.44	–0–
39	33½	32⅞	1,080	.625	33.1875	– .1875	– .56	1,484	73	.438	143	.51	–1.09
40	34⅛	33⅝	4,401	.500	33.875	+ .6875	+2.03	1,750	251	.438	114	2.20	+ .92
41	35¼	33⅞	3,325	1.375	34.5625	+ .6875	+1.99	1,932	172	.525	262	.66	+3.02
42	36¼	35	4,240	1.250	35.625	+1.0625	+2.98	2,172	195	.600	208	.94	+3.17
43	35¼	34⅛	1,702	1.125	34.6875	– .9375	–2.70	2,224	77	.675	167	.46	–5.87
44	35⅞	34⅜	2,009	1.500	35.125	+ .4375	+1.25	2,239	90	.788	190	.47	+2.66
45	36¼	35½	2,569	.750	35.875	+ .750	+2.09	2,390	107	.813	92	1.16	+1.80
46	37	36⅛	2,154	.875	36.5625	+ .6875	+1.88	2,531	85	.875	100	.85	+2.21
47	38⅝	36⅜	2,348	2.250	37.500	+ .9375	+2.50	2,650	89	1.075	209	.43	+5.81
48	39⅜	38¼	3,000	1.125	38.8125	+1.3125	+3.38	2,683	112	1.138	99	1.13	+2.99
49	38¾	37¾	2,292	1.000	38.250	– .5625	–1.47	2,804	84	1.175	85	.96	– .85

Column 4—The volume for that day, expressed as the number of round lots. For example, in the first entry 1,771 means 177,100 shares traded that day.

Column 5—The range for that day. This is the high, expressed as a decimal (column 2), minus the low (column 3), also expressed as a decimal. (First entry: 33.500 − 32.875 = .625)

Figure 18-1
AETNA—DAILY (interval: 50,000 shares)

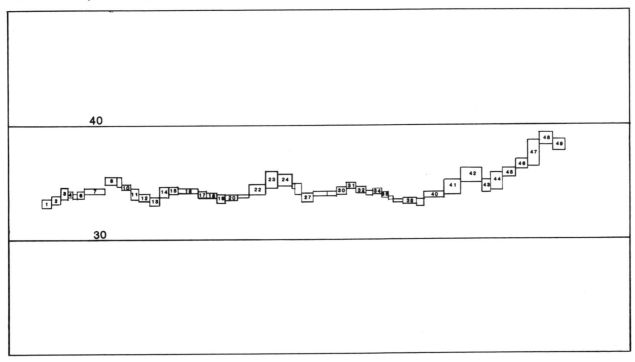

Column 6—The exact midpoint. Calculated by adding the high and the low and dividing by 2. First entry:

$$\frac{33.500 + 32.875}{2} = 33.1875$$

Column 7—The midpoint move. Calculated by subtracting yesterday's midpoint from today's midpoint. (Second entry minus first entry: 33.4375 − 33.1875 = +.250)

Column 8—Here we start to normalize the entries. In order to compare stocks to one another, we must have comparable entries. Therefore we express the midpoint move as a percentage of the price. Our price determinant is that day's midpoint. On day 2, the stock moved up .250 points, as we saw in Column 7. The midpoint on day 2 was 33.437, so the percentage midpoint move was

$$\frac{.250}{33.4375 \times 100} = +.7477,$$

which we can round off to .75, but being careful to retain the plus sign since the moves can be up or down. On that day, the stock moved upward three fourths of 1 percent of its price.

Column 9—Our next chore is to express the volume in such a way that volume variety is retained while stocks are treated equally, regardless of whether they are heavy traders or light traders. To do this, we must have a value with which to compare today's volume, a number that expresses "normal" volume for the stock. We acquire this number by averaging the volume for some period in the recent past. For the sake of this illustration, we have averaged the volume over the last 10 days (column 9). If you are using a computer, we suggest a longer time span, at least 30 days. Since this value is constantly changing, we have, in the process, eliminated any problems that might arise if the stock changes its volume characteristics. Line 10 is the first entry in this column. We see that the value is 1,687; that is, the average volume over the last 10 days was 168,700 shares.

Column 10—Utilizing the results from column 9, we can now arrive at a normalized volume figure. This is accomplished by dividing today's volume by the average volume for the last 10 days and multiplying by 100. On line 10, for example, today's volume was 161,000. Dividing this value by the average of 168,700 and multiplying by 100, we see that on day 10 the volume was 95 percent of normal volume. We now have the first of the two numbers necessary for calculating the box ratio.

Column 11—As with volume, the range of a stock is only meaningful as it compares to normal range. We want to know if today's range is unusually large or unusually small. Consequently, we average the ranges just as we did the volume. In this example, we have used a 10-day average in order to simplify the calculation. With a computer we would use a longer period: Thirty days would be satisfactory. The entry on line 10 of column 11, for example, shows that the average trading range over the last 10 days was .625 points.

Column 12—Similar to column 10, this column compares the current entry to the average entry over the last 10 days. By dividing today's range by the 10-day average range and multiplying by 100, we have today's range expressed as a percentage of the normal range. On line 10 we see

$$\frac{.500}{.625 \times 100} = 80.$$

Day 10's range is 80 percent of normal. We now have developed the second component of the box ratio.

Column 13—Shows the box ratio. As in previous work, it is calculated by dividing the volume by the range. Under our normalized system, we divide the percentage volume (column 10) by the percentage range (column 12). On line 10, this is

$$\frac{.95}{.80} = 1.19.$$

Now we are finally ready to derive the normalized EMV.

Column 14—The normalized EMV. It is calculated, as before, by dividing the midpoint move by the box ratio. We, of course, use the normalized values in columns 8 and 13. So, following across on line 10, we obtain the normalized EMV:

$$-1.26 \div 1.19 \times -1.06.$$

Table 18–2 represents the last series of steps, the calculation of the 13-day moving average of the EMV, and the change-of-direction notations. Now we have produced results very similar to our previous work, but with the additional advantage of being able to compare one stock to another. A stronger 13-day EMV indicates a stock that is moving more powerfully. With these numbers, we are able to sort out the stocks that are more likely to show us rapid profits. It is an improvement on the nonnormalized numbers, but calls for very time-consuming calculations and is more suited to data-processing equipment.

Table 18–2
AETNA EMVs (13-DAY)

Day	Normalized EMV	13-Day EMV	Change
10	−1.06		
11	−4.18		
12	− .61		
13	+ .55		
14	+1.10		
15	+ .37		
16	−0−		
17	− .59		
18	− .29		
19	− .73		
20	−0−		
21	+ .22		
22	+1.65	− 3.57	
23	+5.51	+ 3.00	Up
24	− .26	+ 6.92	Up
25	−6.48	+ 1.05	Down
26	−1.36	− .86	Down
27	−1.72	− 3.68	Down
28	+ .23	− 3.82	Down*
29	+ .14	− 3.68	Up
30	+ .86	− 2.23	Up
31	+1.09	− .85	Up
32	− .88	− 1.00	Down
33	− .96	− 1.96	Down
34	+ .54	− 1.64	Down
35	−2.26	− 5.55	Down*
36	− .91	−11.97	Down
37	− .64	−12.35	Down
38	−0−	− 5.87	Up
39	−1.09	− 5.60	Up
40	+ .92	− 2.96	Up
41	+3.02	− .17	Up†
42	+3.17	+ 2.86	Up
43	−5.87	− 3.87	Down
44	+2.66	− 2.30	Up
45	+1.80	+ .38	Up
46	+2.21	+ 3.55	Up
47	+5.81	+ 8.82	Up†
48	+2.99	+14.47	Up
49	− .85	+14.53	Up

* Four consecutive downs—the signal to sell.
† Four consecutive ups—the signal that the stock has reversed to the upside.

Chapter 19   Ease of Movement—Indices

Knowing the general market direction is an important consideration in investment strategy. Our prior work on EMV for individual stocks tells us quite reliably when to buy or sell any given issue. Market direction acts as a confirmation, however. Buying a stock in a down market may turn out to be profitable, but we are more likely to be correct and the moves are more likely to be substantial if we are in tune with the market. Consequently, it is worthwhile to follow the EMV for the overall market as well as the individual issues.

In the following examples, we have reproduced the charts and EMV for the Dow Jones industrials on both a weekly and a daily basis. Other indices, such as Standard & Poor's 500 or the New York Stock Exchange, could be used if ranges were readily available. Most publications, however, only show closing values for these indices, eliminating a price range, which is, of course, a key element in our EMV calculations. The range for the Dow Jones industrials is published daily in *The Wall Street Journal* and many other newspapers. This is an intraday figure, representing the absolute highs and lows of all of the component issues during that trading day, regardless of when during the day they occurred.

Figures 19–1, 19–2, and 19–3 show the weekly postings of the Dow Jones industrials in the years 1979, 1980, and 1981. During this time, the market went through an indecisive series of swings, then a major advance, and finally a major decline. Table 19–1 shows the results of our EMV calculations for that period.

Looking at the 13-week EMV values and observing the points where they go from plus to minus or minus to plus, we see a large number of signals, including one that lasts for only a week. We see that they would have been helpful in recognizing the major moves, but that they produced a number of whipsaws also. During the top in late 1980 and early 1981, a number of signals were generated which could have been costly before the sell signal at the beginning of the major decline. On the other hand, utilizing the four-week reversal (marked by asterisks on the table) would have been much more effective. Combining these signals with EMV information on individual issues could have been very profitable.

Figure 19–4 and Table 19–2 show the results of using the daily rather than the weekly figures over a much shorter time span. The period mid-July to mid-August of 1982 was an indecisive period, with the market looking for a bottom. As a result, the 13-week EMV was erratic and gave a number of signals before the buy signal at August 17, which was the beginning of a substantial advance.

As can be seen from these examples, the work on indices is not as reliable as on individual stocks, but it can help us to make sure we are not on the

Figure 19–1
DOW JONES INDUSTRIALS—WEEKLY (1979)

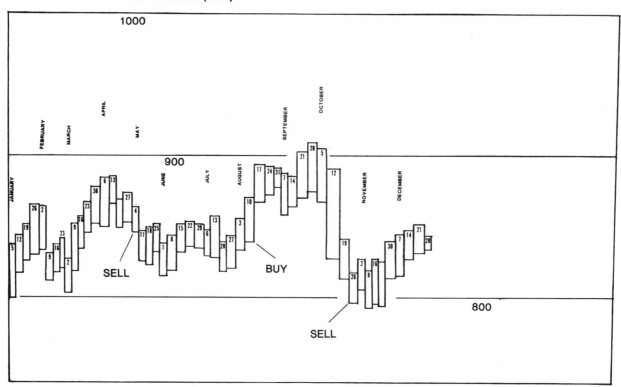

Figure 19–2
DOW JONES INDUSTRIALS—WEEKLY (1980)

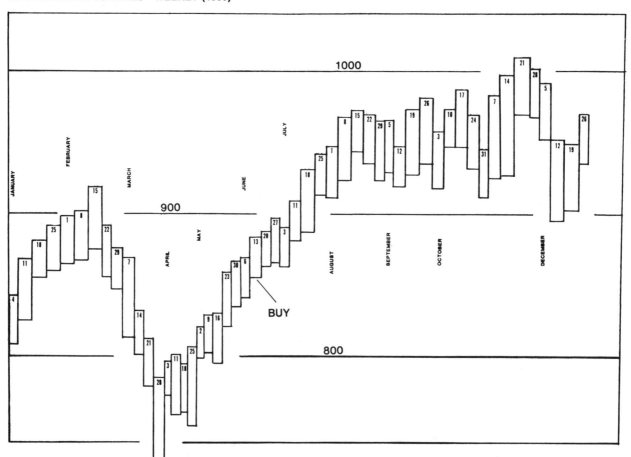

Figure 19–3
DOW JONES INDUSTRIALS—WEEKLY (1981)

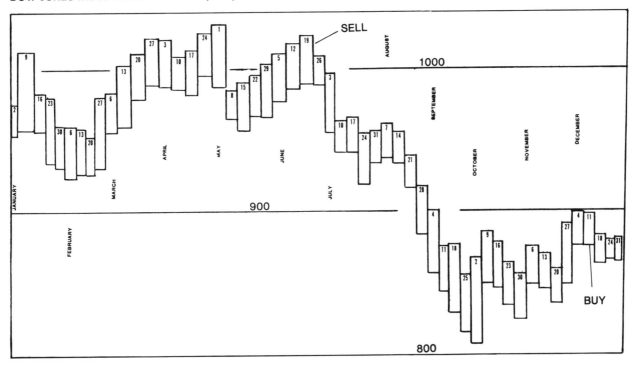

Table 19–1
DOW JONES INDUSTRIALS—WEEKLY

Date	Ease of movement	13-Day ease of movement	Change
1/12/79	+ 23.91		
1/19/79	+ 17.39		
1/26/79	+ 20.45		
2/02/79	+ 2.50		
2/09/79	− 45.00		
2/16/79	+ 10.00		
2/23/79	+ 7.50		
3/02/79	− 24.00		
3/09/79	+ 47.50		
3/16/79	+ 22.00		
3/23/79	+ 20.37		
3/30/79	+ 12.90		
4/06/79	+ 4.17	+119.69	
4/13/79	+ 15.00	+110.79	Down
4/20/79	− 26.67	+ 66.72	Down
4/27/79	+ 3.75	+ 50.02	Down
5/04/79	− 12.12	+ 35.40	Down*
5/11/79	− 31.67	+ 48.73	Up
5/18/79	−0−	+ 38.73	Down
5/25/79	+ 7.58	+ 38.81	Up
6/01/79	− 27.78	+ 35.03	Down
6/08/79	+ 7.58	− 4.89	Down
6/15/79	+ 13.75	− 13.14	Down
6/22/79	+ 3.41	− 30.10	Down*
6/29/79	− 2.00	− 45.00	Down
7/06/79	− 6.06	− 55.23	Down
7/13/79	+ 7.41	− 62.82	Down
7/20/79	− 23.33	− 59.48	Up
7/27/79	+ 4.17	− 59.06	Up
8/03/79	+ 18.06	− 28.88	Up
8/10/79	+ 18.52	+ 21.31	Up†

Table 19–1 *(continued)*

Date	Ease of movement	13-Day ease of movement	Change
8/17/79	+ 41.94	+ 63.25	Up
8/24/79	+ 2.50	+ 58.17	Down
8/31/79	+ 2.33	+ 88.28	Up
9/07/79	− 30.00	+ 50.70	Down
9/14/79	+ 2.78	+ 39.73	Down
9/21/79	+ 17.74	+ 54.06	Up
9/28/79	+ 12.50	+ 68.56	Up
10/05/79	− 14.29	+ 60.33	Down
10/12/79	− 71.05	− 18.13	Down
10/19/79	− 53.33	− 48.13	Down
10/26/79	− 25.00	− 77.30	Down*
11/02/79	+ 18.52	− 76.84	Up
11/09/79	− 23.91	−119.27	Down
11/16/82	+ 15.80	−145.41	Down
11/23/79	− 2.63	−150.54	Down
11/30/79	+ 25.81	−127.06	Up
12/07/79	+ 7.41	− 89.65	Up
12/14/79	+ 7.50	− 84.93	Up
12/21/79	+ 5.00	− 97.97	Down
12/28/79	− 2.50	−112.67	Down
1/04/80	− 27.08	−125.46	Down
1/11/80	+ 36.21	− 18.20	Up
1/18/80	+ 25.00	+ 60.13	Up
1/25/80	+ 7.50	+ 92.63	Up
2/01/80	+ 7.89	+ 82.00	Down
2/08/80	+ 2.86	+108.77	Up
2/15/80	+ 22.41	+115.38	Up
2/22/80	− 47.92	+ 70.09	Down
2/29/80	− 16.67	+ 27.61	Down
3/07/80	− 52.63	− 32.43	Down
3/14/80	− 46.30	− 86.23	Down*
3/21/80	− 42.00	−133.23	Down
3/28/80	−100.00	−230.73	Down
4/03/80	+ 54.00	−149.65	Up
4/11/80	− 10.53	−196.39	Down
4/18/80	− 5.56	−226.95	Down
4/25/80	+ 3.57	−230.88	Down
5/02/80	+ 50.00	−188.77	Up
5/09/80	+ 9.68	−181.95	Up
5/16/80	− 4.17	−208.53	Down
5/23/80	+ 64.29	− 96.32	Up
5/30/80	+ 18.52	− 61.13	Up
6/06/80	+ 6.90	− 1.60	Up
6/13/80	+ 19.44	+ 64.14	Up†
6/20/80	+ 10.61	+116.75	Up
6/27/80	+ 9.26	+226.01	Up
7/03/80	− 3.45	+168.56	Down
7/11/80	+ 22.37	+201.46	Up
7/18/80	+ 25.86	+232.88	Up
7/25/80	+ 25.00	+254.31	Up
8/01/80	+ 1.79	+206.10	Down
8/05/80	+ 37.78	+234.20	Up
8/15/80	+ 16.17	+254.54	Up
8/22/80	− 5.17	+185.08	Down
8/29/80	− 31.58	+134.98	Down
9/05/80	+ 11.36	+139.44	Up
9/12/80	− 19.44	+100.56	Down
9/19/80	+ 32.69	+122.64	Up
9/26/80	+ 15.38	+128.76	Up
10/03/80	− 40.00	+ 92.21	Down
10/10/80	+ 28.95	+ 98.79	Up
10/17/80	+ 14.00	+ 86.93	Down
10/24/80	− 32.69	+ 29.24	Down
10/31/80	− 44.00	− 16.55	Down

Table 19–1 *(concluded)*

Date	Ease of movement	13-Day ease of movement	Change
11/07/80	+ 76.47	+ 22.14	Up
11/14/80	+ 29.41	+ 35.38	Up
11/21/80	+ 34.29	+ 74.84	Up
11/28/80	− 8.00	+ 98.42	Up†
12/05/80	− 25.00	+ 62.06	Down
12/12/80	−114.29	− 32.79	Down
12/19/80	+ 1.92	− 63.56	Down
12/26/80	+ 61.36	− 17.58	Up
1/02/81	+ 24.07	+ 46.49	Up
1/09/81	+ 40.00	+ 57.54	Up
1/16/81	− 19.74	+ 23.80	Down
1/23/81	− 32.35	+ 24.14	Up
1/30/81	− 20.37	+ 47.77	Up
2/06/81	− 7.14	− 35.84	Down
2/13/81	−0−	− 65.25	Down
2/20/81	− 1.61	−101.15	Down
2/27/81	+ 37.50	− 55.65	Up
3/06/81	+ 19.44	− 11.21	Up
3/13/81	+ 20.37	+123.45	Up
3/20/81	+ 18.42	+139.95	Up†
3/27/81	+ 14.47	+ 93.06	Down
4/03/81	− 3.45	+ 65.54	Down
4/10/81	− 6.36	+ 19.18	Down
4/17/81	−0−	+ 38.92	Up
4/24/81	+ 16.25	+ 87.52	Up
5/01/81	− 1.85	+106.04	Up
5/08/81	− 34.00	+ 79.18	Down
5/15/81	− 3.45	+ 75.73	Down
5/22/81	+ 11.11	+ 88.45	Up
5/29/81	+ 5.36	+ 56.31	Down
6/05/81	+ 14.29	+ 51.16	Down
6/12/81	+ 8.75	+ 39.54	Down
6/19/81	+ 4.29	+ 25.41	Down*
6/26/81	− 6.00	− 4.94	Down
7/03/81	− 57.50	− 49.11	Down
7/10/81	− 23.00	− 65.75	Down
7/17/81	+ 1.11	− 64.64	Up
7/24/81	− 28.57	−109.46	Down
7/31/81	+ 9.52	− 98.09	Up
8/07/81	+ 4.76	− 59.33	Up
8/14/81	− 4.44	− 60.32	Down
8/21/81	− 20.00	− 91.43	Down
8/28/81	− 44.83	−141.62	Down
9/04/81	− 50.00	−205.91	Down*
9/11/81	− 36.00	−250.66	Down
9/18/81	− 18.18	−273.13	Down
9/25/81	− 34.00	−301.13	Down
10/02/81	+ 5.88	−237.75	Up
10/09/81	+ 53.57	−161.18	Up
10/16/81	− 10.00	−172.29	Down
10/23/81	− 21.21	−164.93	Up
10/30/81	− 13.64	−188.09	Down
11/06/81	+ 23.91	−168.94	Up
11/13/81	− 4.76	−169.26	Down
11/20/81	− 11.90	−161.16	Up
11/27/81	+ 57.89	− 58.44	Up
12/04/81	+ 17.78	+ 9.34	Up
12/11/81	−0−	+ 45.34	Up†
12/18/81	− 12.00	+ 51.52	Up
12/24/81	− .75	+ 84.77	Up
12/31/81	−0−	+ 78.89	Down

* Four consecutive downs—the signal to sell.
† Four consecutive ups—the signal that the stock has reversed to the upside.

Figure 19–4
DOW JONES INDUSTRIALS—DAILY

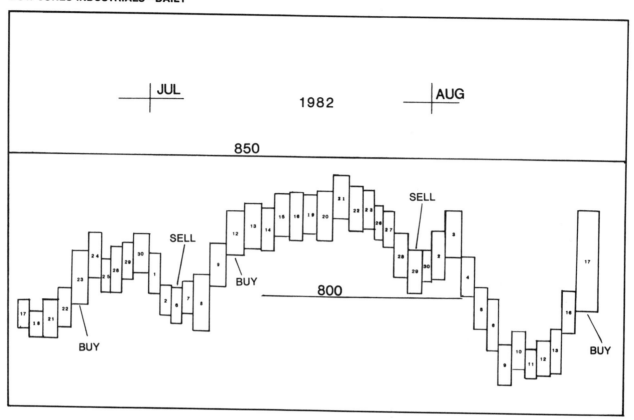

Table 19–2
DOW JONES INDUSTRIALS—DAILY

Date	Ease of movement	13-Day ease of movement	Change
6/17/82	−16.1	− 77.6	Down
6/18/82	− 4.7	− 71.2	Up
6/21/82	+ 3.3	− 65.7	Up
6/22/82	+10.5	− 57.8	Up
6/23/82	+28.4	− 8.2	Up*
6/24/82	+19.8	+ 30.0	Up
6/25/82	−20.8	+ 8.2	Down
6/28/82	+ 6.1	+ 30.6	Up
6/29/82	+ 7.9	+ 38.5	Up
6/30/82	+ 5.6	+ 21.7	Down
7/01/82	−21.2	+ 12.7	Down
7/02/82	−19.0	+ 4.8	Down
7/06/82	− 5.6	− 5.8	Down†
7/07/82	+ 7.1	+ 17.4	Up
7/08/82	− 4.1	+ 18.0	Up
7/09/82	+27.0	+ 41.7	Up
7/12/82	+21.7	+ 52.9	Up*
7/13/82	+ 4.3	+ 28.8	Down
7/14/82	− 4.1	+ 4.9	Down
7/15/82	+13.8	+ 45.6	Up
7/16/82	−0−	+ 39.5	Down
7/19/82	+ 2.2	+ 33.8	Down
7/20/82	− 2.4	+ 25.8	Down
7/21/82	+17.0	+ 64.0	Up
7/22/82	−10.5	+ 72.5	Up
7/23/82	− 1.3	+ 76.8	Up
7/26/82	−12.9	+ 56.8	Down

Table 19–2 *(concluded)*

Date	Ease of movement	13-Day ease of movement	Change
7/27/82	− 7.9	+ 53.0	Down
7/28/82	−22.5	+ 1.5	Down
7/29/82	−18.2	− 38.4	Down†
7/30/82	+ 6.3	− 36.4	Up
8/02/82	+ 8.8	− 23.5	Up
8/03/82	+17.0	− 20.3	Up
8/04/82	−34.9	− 55.2	Down
8/05/82	−25.6	− 83.0	Down
8/06/82	−22.4	−103.0	Down
8/09/82	−31.4	−151.4	Down†
8/10/82	+11.6	−129.3	Up
8/11/82	−10.0	−138.0	Down
8/12/82	+ 4.0	−121.1	Up
8/13/82	+ 7.6	−105.6	Up
8/16/82	+33.8	− 49.3	Up
8/17/82	+66.7	+ 35.6	Up*
8/18/82	+64.8	+ 94.1	Up

* Four consecutive ups—the signal that the stock has reversed to the upside.
† Four consecutive downs—the signal to sell.

wrong side of the market during its larger moves. The reason it is less helpful is that it represents a large number of stocks. Consequently, there is a smoothing effect that makes the entries look more alike. There is not as much volume variety nor as dramatic price moves. The EMV work, therefore, loses some of its strengths. It is the shape of the boxes that modifies the price moves in our EMV work. On the basis of a market index, there is very little difference between easy movement and difficult movement. We advise watching the EMV on the overall market, but using it as a confirmation of other work rather than a signal demanding action.

Part Four   Putting It All Together

Chapter 20   The Trader's Attitude

Every technique illustrated in this book is useless if a trader does not have the right attitude. Success in the market calls for three essential ingredients: a valid technique, a detached attitude, and a willingness to do the work. The techniques are here, but the other two factors must be contributed by the reader.

To be successful, a trader (or an investor) must have a detached attitude toward the market. He must be able to stand back and look at himself looking at the market, and critically appraise his actions. His emotions are his worst enemies, unless they are understood and controlled. Understanding our own emotions necessitates the understanding of the emotionalism of the marketplace.

Every time a stock changes hands, two emotions are at work—fear and greed. The buyer is expecting to make a profit and is motivated by that desire. The seller fears either that he will lose what profit he has or that his losses will get worse. He has reached the point when fear has overcome the original greed which motivated him to take the position. Of these two emotions, fear is the more powerful. In buying a stock there is less emotional involvement, since until that point the trader has had no money involved. As soon as he buys the stock, however, he is emotionally involved. His money is in there and it is at the mercy of the fluctuating marketplace. As a result, buys (or shorts) tend to be objective decisions, while sells (or covering of shorts) tend to be emotional decisions.

Emotional decisions are bad decisions. Fear and greed are the enemies that must be overcome if one is to succeed in the stock market, and this calls for an objective approach to the market. Decisions must be made in accordance with set rules, not based on overwhelming fear or greed. Some people should not be stock market traders, because they are unable to overcome their emotions. From the standpoint of the unemotional market operator, it is helpful that these emotional participants are there, however. Often we will be buying from them when they are liquidating in a blind panic. At other times, we will be selling to them when they are afraid they will miss the boat.

There are five rules for overcoming emotionalism and maintaining objectivity:

1. *Have a system in which you believe.* Confidence is the key here. Whether it be the system in this book or another system you develop yourself, it must be a complete and reliable discipline. It should have rules for buying and rules for selling, and they must be well-defined rules that cannot be ignored. In addition, it is important not to try to combine systems or use more than one. If a stock is bought on technical signals, it should not be sold on the basis of fundamentals. In fact, a good technician should shield

himself from outside influences that are not a part of his system; otherwise, he is likely to be influenced by outside information and make an emotional decision. Reading every market letter, following the news, listening to six different brokers, and talking to other traders lead only to confusion. The stock market is telling a story. Listen to that story, as related in terms of price and volume, know the rules, and act accordingly.

2. *Forget the money.* This is hard to do, of course, but the trader must forget that money represents buying power. If he thinks of money as a new car, a mink coat, or a swimming pool, he has upped his emotional involvement and is less likely to make rational decisions. He must use money to keep score only. A good way of accomplishing this is to set a rule whereby profits may not be withdrawn and used. All of the money placed in stocks is to be used only for playing the game and is never to leave the brokerage account. In this way, it ceases to have any meaning outside of the market and can be treated more objectively.

Another help is figuring profits or losses in percentages rather than dollars. This technique removes some of the fear and greed. It becomes a contest to see if the gains can be made to exceed the losses. Your objective should be to make a certain percentage per month or per year, rather than to make a certain number of dollars.

3. *Keep records.* We don't mean just records for the IRS, although they are also important. We mean keep an accurate journal of every move you make or *don't* make in the market. Upon considering buying a stock (or shorting one), write down all of the reasons for making the move. Using a trader's check list, such as the one in Chapter 24, is one way of doing this. After buying a stock, write a justification for the purchase. Review the stock often and write down the reasons you are still holding it. If it does not act as you expected, write down why and show the reasons you are still holding the position. Finally, when you get out of a position, show why you did so. Be very critical of yourself. If you take a loss, find out where you went wrong and, just as important, if you take a profit, analyze what you did correctly.

Postmortems are not only allowed—they are necessary. After you close out a position, check back from time to time to see if you did the right thing. It is popular, after getting out of a stock, to say, "Never look back." We say look back and be critical. This is a way of learning.

4. *Keep it to yourself.* The stock market makes interesting cocktail party conversation, but conversation does you no good. As soon as you tell anyone what you own, you have introduced an extraneous factor to your decision-making process. It now matters whether you are right or wrong in another's eyes. It makes it that much harder to take a loss when the rules say the stock should be sold. Wishful thinking takes the place of reason, and you should allow no room for wishful thinking.

5. *Limit the number of positions.* Owning a large number of stocks contains two pitfalls. First is the fact that one does not have a big enough ownership in any of them to constitute a disaster if they go against one. It makes it too easy to ignore a bad situation because it only represents one small part of the portfolio. This can lead to kidding oneself about a stock that is down because the loss is offset by another stock that is up. Portfolios are for long-term investors, not for traders.

Second, it is difficult to watch a larger number of positions as intently as we recommend. If you follow our advice on record keeping, you cannot keep up with a large number of holdings. Unless a large amount of money is involved, whereby the trader may be influencing the very market he is trying to trade, it may be wise to own only one stock at a time. In this way there can be no rationalizations. We suggest, however, keeping charts on a fairly large number of stocks in order to recognize opportunities when they arise. They should be stocks that trade quite heavily and that have a history of worthwhile price swings.

All of the above rules add up to the golden rule of trading: *Don't kid yourself.* You must be an objective investor, divorced from the emotionalism of the marketplace. There is no room for an ego.

The third ingredient to success, as we have said, is a willingness to work at it. Posting charts, keeping records, and analyzing results all call for time and labor. If you are not willing to do that work, you might just as well buy stocks on hot tips or research reports. The work must be yours, if you wish to succeed. Your broker does not have the time or the inclination—and often not the knowledge—to make these decisions for you.

Stock market trading is a business and should be approached in a business-like manner. Decisions should be based on logic, not emotions. There are thousands of emotional market participants out there waiting to take losses, and these losses can be the serious trader's gains.

Chapter 21   Combining EMV and Cycles— Daily Charts

Throughout the book we have seen a number of different adaptations of Equivolume. Now it is time to put them together and see how they can confirm one another and lead us to more profitable market decisions. Assuming in this chapter that we are aggressive market traders, we will work with a daily chart of a very volatile stock and will try to apply all of the techniques we have learned.

Figure 21–1 shows about five months of trading activity in Federal Express during 1982. We have numbered the boxes from 16 to 124. The first 15 boxes are not shown since it takes those days to build up the information necessary to develop the EMV numbers and their 13-day moving average.

The progress of the analysis should follow the format of the book. We should look first at box shapes, then at formations, next at wave patterns, and finally at ease of movement.

We see that day 17 is a square day, within what is evidently a tight trading area. The stock is having difficulty moving up or down. One day 23, however, it breaks out decisively to the downside, implying extreme weakness and suggesting a short sale. On day 27, it again goes square as it reaches a support level. The next day, as it moves up, it finds upside movement to be equally difficult as it goes square again. Day 30 confirms the weakness as it moves very easily to the downside. The next rally (32 to 35) is off a low-volume bottom and does not look convincing. After further weakness, we see day 44, an oversquare day, which may be indicating a more important area of support. The sideways move from day 44 to day 52 is penetrated on the upside on day 53. In addition, the move is enough to penetrate a descending trend line. Day 55 is again a square, showing difficulty of upside movement, and it follows a gap that looks like an exhaustion gap. At this point, it looks as though the stock will pull back, but the lack of any width to the top says that the pullback is likely to be shallow. Much more important is the fact that the trend has definitely turned up. At 59, we see that the low is above the prior lows at day 44 and day 51, encouraging us to remain bullish on the stock. The pullback to day 73 is again higher and would seem to still be within a broad upward trend, but would certainly be worrisome.

The square at 75 should get our attention. The stock is having trouble moving. It does penetrate this level, going up to box 81. There is little clue to this being a top except that the stock is at the top of its channel. At 88, however, decided weakness comes in, which penetrates the uptrend line on easy movement.

There is a consolidation area between 92 and 100 that may be only temporary support, or may lead to a turnaround. We see a tightening between the buyers and the sellers, and should be looking for a decisive move in

Figure 21–1
FEDERAL EXPRESS—DAILY (interval: 50,000 shares)

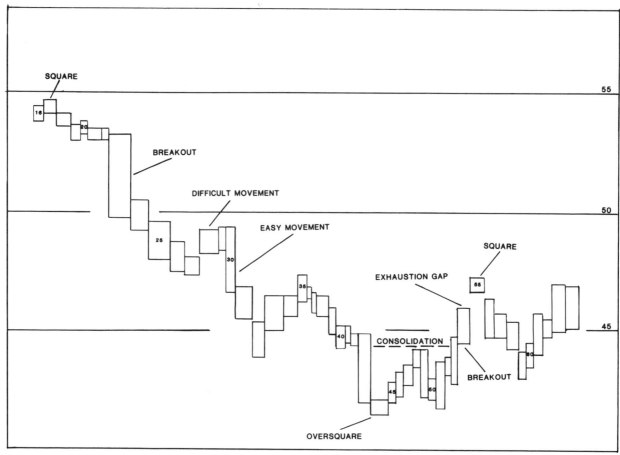

one direction or the other. Day 100 shows a penetration of the descending trend line, implying an upward move. Day 106 is square, as the stock meets resistance at the old highs at 81. Days 111 and 114 show a reluctance to move upward. The stock is losing momentum. The area between 111 and 116 is another consolidation, which is broken on the downside at 118 and says the stock is going lower.

These box and formation signals certainly would have been helpful in trading the stock. Perhaps, however, we could eliminate some of the uncertainties by looking at the cycles and EMV work. Figure 21–2 shows the same stock, but here we have outlined the minor and intermediate channels and also indicated the buy and sell points as they were generated by the crossovers of the 13-day moving average of the EMV. Table 21–1 shows the calculated values of the 13-day EMV.

A very regular rhythm can be seen in the way the minor channel approaches the limits of the intermediate channel. These points have been shown by the arrows that appear across the lower margin of the chart. The width of the intermediate channel was well established during the downmove from day 16 to 50, and 53 forced us to turn the channel upward, indicating a change of direction. Day 59, based only on box shapes, might have caused us some consternation; it was obviously in the area where we would expect a low, considering our cyclical work, and this factor would have kept us from closing out a long position. The same thing happens at day 73. The stock has returned to the bottom of the channel but has not penetrated it, and a low is due. We would be inclined to stay long. Day 88 is a different

Figure 21–1 *(concluded)*

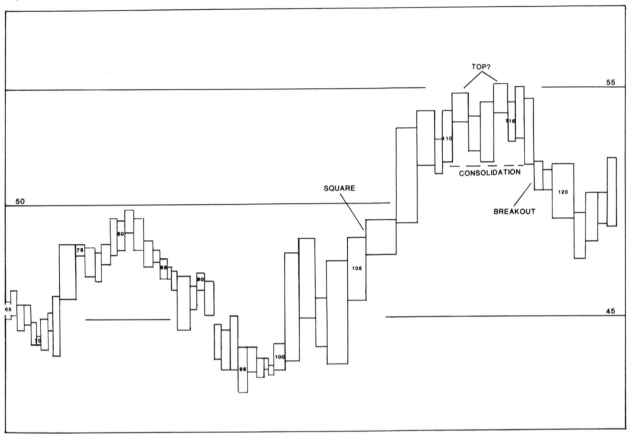

situation. It comes where expected, but is too low. It forces a curving downward of the intermediate channel, and we would expect a rally because it is cyclically due, but we would be inclined to sell as soon as possible. The square day at 90, the bottom of the prior consolidation, would be that opportunity.

Day 101 again forces our intermediate channel upward, indicating the stock should be bought. We know, however, that the stock is due for a minor cycle low very shortly, and suspect that we may be near the top of the upward channel even though the stock has turned up. The cycles might keep us from buying immediately, waiting for the cyclic low, which does occur at day 104. Finally, day 119 again forces our intermediate channel downward and should prompt us to be sellers.

The EMV numbers (Table 21–1) had some very good signals and some less helpful signals. Following them blindly would have produced very good profits overall, but we would have had some small losses that might have been avoided.

The first sell, at day 22, recognized the weakness in the stock before the downside breakout and led to a very profitable move. The buy at day 54 would confirm the beginning of the upside move spotted by the cycles, the consolidation, and the trend lines. The sell at day 59 was not good. Taken alone, it would have led to a loss. There are other considerations, however. Following cycles, we expected a low in this area, and our trend was definitely up, based on the intermediate wave. We would tend to override the 13-sell at this point and stay long, in view of our other information.

Day 67 produces another sell that, if obeyed, would lead to a small profit on the next buy, at 72. It is more likely, however, that we would also choose

Figure 21–2
FEDERAL EXPRESS—DAILY (interval: 50,000 shares)

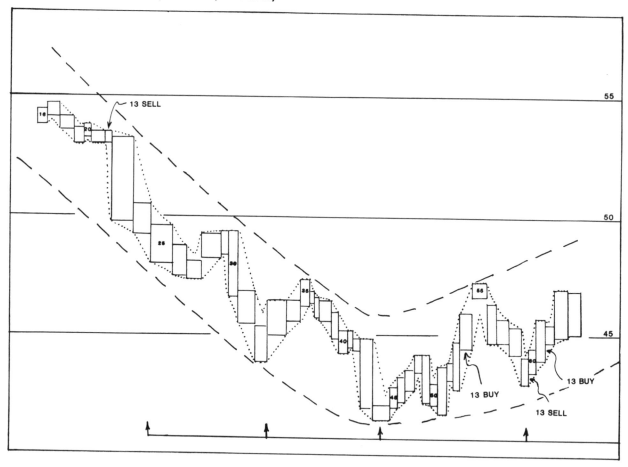

to ignore this signal because of the uptrend in the stock. Had we acted on that signal, however, we would be once again told to buy on day 72, a signal that would lead to a substantial profit prior to the sell at day 86.

The sell at day 86 is the earliest indication of the downmove. Box shapes had told us nothing. Cycles and trend lines had not yet given a signal. It was the first warning that the stock was going lower.

The 13-day EMV gives us a strong buy signal at day 101. This is confirmed by all our other technical work, although the cycle studies would have helped us to buy cheaper, on the pullback. It is a very profitable upward move. The sell at day 120 is a little later than our other indicators, which would have had us out on day 118.

As can be seen, all of the methods and indicators we have introduced are useful, allowing profitable trading. By combining them, however, results can be enhanced. There is no order of precedence in using them. Usually they will confirm one another, with one method having a little lead time over another. All should be utilized, and judgments should be made by studying the stock in each of these ways.

If the box shapes, the cycles, the trend lines, and so forth are all saying the same thing but the EMV is not, check the EMV numbers and see how close you are to a crossover. Note the numbers to be offset in the 13-day moving average over the next few days. It is likely that the EMV will soon follow the other information. Conflicts between signals can usually be clarified by a closer scrutiny. The stock is telling a story, and all we have to do is listen carefully to what it has to say.

Figure 21–2 *(concluded)*

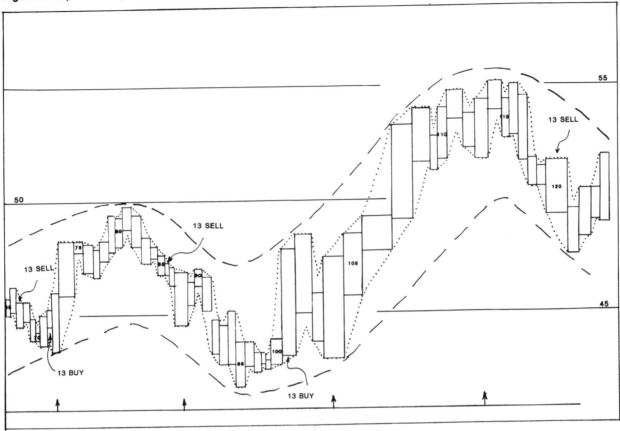

Table 21–1
FEDERAL EXPRESS TRADING

Day	13-Day ease of movement	Day	13-Day ease of movement	Day	13-Day ease of movement
16	+103.5	53	−21.2	90	− 14.5
17	+ 75.8	54	+ 4.4	91	− 40.6
18	+ 53.1	55	+18.3	92	−126.7
19	+ 47.9	56	+26.0	93	−138.7
20	+ 51.7	57	+31.3	94	−133.1
21	+ 57.9	58	+13.4	95	−158.6
22	− 5.8	59	−15.9	96	−134.7
23	− 66.3	60	−12.8	97	−141.0
24	− 88.3	61	+ 0.3	98	−127.5
25	− 85.5	62	+30.7	99	−128.2
26	− 92.2	63	+60.6	100	−110.7
27	− 96.8	64	+55.9	101	+ 37.7
28	− 89.8	65	+19.5	102	+ 73.7
29	− 91.0	66	+16.5	103	+115.1
30	−131.2	67	−27.2	104	+147.3
31	−151.2	68	−36.2	105	+246.2
32	−175.7	69	−26.7	106	+267.6
33	−164.3	70	−26.4	107	+378.5
34	−160.0	71	−12.8	108	+447.5
35	−146.4	72	+23.6	109	+415.5
36	− 90.3	73	− 1.3	110	+454.3
37	− 82.3	74	+28.7	111	+465.6
38	− 72.9	75	+32.2	112	+447.9
39	− 78.9	76	+ 5.1	113	+440.7
40	− 86.9	77	− 2.9	114	+353.1
41	− 91.8	78	+23.2	115	+272.6

Table 21–1 *(concluded)*

Day	13-Day ease of movement	Day	13-Day ease of movement	Day	13-Day ease of movement
42	− 97.1	79	+41.7	116	+232.8
43	−101.4	80	+58.6	117	+180.6
44	− 88.1	81	+66.3	118	+102.9
45	− 46.7	82	+79.8	119	+ 88.9
46	− 53.5	83	+67.6	120	− 46.1
47	− 50.8	84	+59.5	121	−127.1
48	− 53.4	85	+35.4	122	− 76.0
49	− 82.7	86	+48.0	123	− 99.5
50	− 83.4	87	−14.7	124	− 81.4
51	− 76.0	88	−47.2		
52	− 42.7	89	−33.2		

Chapter 22   Combining EMV and Cycles—Weekly Charts

In the last chapter we were looking at a volatile stock, charted on a daily basis, and using it as a trading vehicle. The longer-term investor may not want to utilize such quick moves and would feel more comfortable with longer-term positions. To do this, he should keep weekly charts, but apply all of the same methods demonstrated in the prior chapter.

Figure 22–1 is a weekly-based chart of J. C. Penney during 1980 and the first half of 1981. The numbering of the weeks starts with the 17th, since it was necessary to accumulate some information that does not appear on the chart in order to have EMV-13 numbers.

We see that there is a good variety of box shapes and box sizes even though this is a weekly chart. The stock has a tendency to form square boxes on tops and bottoms, with easier movement in between.

The chart history consists of two advances and one decline, all of large enough magnitude to be usable by a longer-term investor. Each move lasted approximately four months, and the average move during these three periods was approximately 35 percent of the price of the stock.

Looking at box shapes and formations, the first part of our analysis, we see a decline in progress from weeks 17 through 24. Week 25 is unusually square and is a change from the easy movement that precedes it. There would be no reason to buy at this time, since it was only a possible end to the decline. Before buying, we want to see a consolidation and a breakout to the upside, with a favorable box shape on the breakout. In addition, we are looking for a wide enough consolidation to justify a substantial move. On week 25, we only know that the stock has found temporary support; even after a consolidation, the move could just as easily be a continuation downward.

The stock does build a small sideways area between weeks 25 and 31, and then breaks out to the upside with easy movement on week 32. When we measure the width of the consolidation (A–B) and project the move to point C, it appears that the move may not go far, and we would probably be reluctant to buy the stock. Assuming we decided to follow the move, however, and were long, we would now be looking for a reason to take profits. Our objective, in terms of volume, would be at C. There is nothing in the box shapes to tell us the move has terminated in the 40 area, and a trend line would not take us out either. Week 49, however, indicates a turning sideways of the stock and would force us to take profits if we had not done so already, based on the projected objective.

As we moved across the top toward week 54, we would become aware that a large consolidation was forming. The square lows and spike highs would lead us to suspect that the next move would be up; but, abiding by the rules, we would not buy the stock during a consolidation. Week 54 justifies

Figure 22-1
J. C. PENNEY—WEEKLY (interval: 200,000 shares)

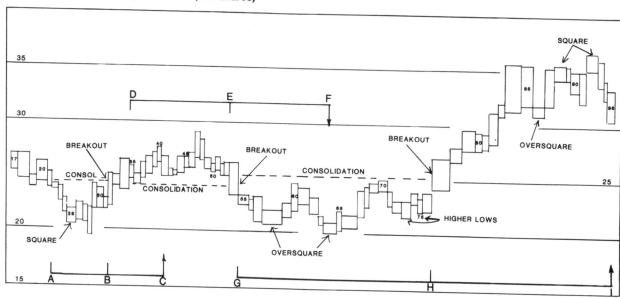

our caution as the stock breaks out to the downside with increasing volume and a widening of the spread.

Measuring the width of the consolidation, we could see that distance D–E justified a drop to the vicinity of F, and a short position would be justified. After almost a month on the downside, week 58 would certainly give us pause, and we might be inclined to cover the short positions due to its oversquare nature. If we had the nerve to stay with it, however, we would get another oversquare at 64 that did satisfy our volume objective, and we would then take our profits.

At week 64, we have no position. The downward move appears to have ended, but so far we have no indication of the future direction of movement. We would do nothing in the stock between weeks 64 and 77. We would merely observe the wide consolidation pattern, with squares at the highs and lows, knowing that the next move out of such a wide consolidation could be quite profitable.

Week 77 could leave no doubt in our minds. The volume and range were very impressive and there was even a breakaway gap. Projecting the probable move, we would measure G to H and project a top at I. The move did carry well to the vicinity of our objective, with one bothersome week at 86. Its squareness implied good support but may have been telling us the upward move was coming to an end. The squares at week 88 and 92 would have confirmed this contention and would also have satisfied our objective.

Weeks 88 to 91 appeared to be another consolidation, again alerting us to a new opportunity. The move above the resistance at 92 was not believable, however, because of its squareness.

Let us now move on to Figure 22–2, which shows the same stock again, but this time with the waves outlined and the EMV signals entered.

We can see that the stock has a good cyclic pattern, and have indicated with arrows at the bottom of the page the areas where the minor cycle approaches the intermediate channel. This information would have been helpful a number of times in following the signals given by the boxes and formations.

At week 64, where we were considering covering shorts, we would have seen that a cyclic low was due, which would reinforce our decision to act.

Figure 22-2
J. C. PENNEY—WEEKLY (interval: 200,000 shares)

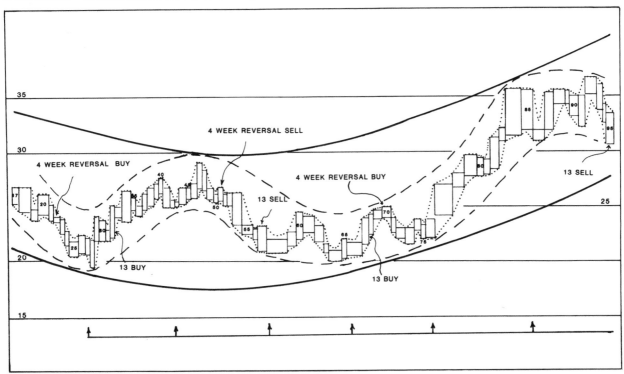

The low at 76 would indicate that we were just beginning an upward cycle and would confirm our decision to buy on week 77. The perplexing low on week 86 would make more sense, since a low was due at that time. Finally, the false breakout at week 92 would be even more suspect because it came midway in the cycle, making it difficult to expect more of an advance at that time.

Looking at the intermediate channel, we see that it is forced downward well in advance of the break at week 54, avoiding overstaying the long position. Later, it is forced upward at week 67, warning us that the next move would be to the upside. The contention was well confirmed by the higher bottoms at 73 and 76. At box 95, the stock should, according to the cycles in the minor wave, be approaching a low. On the other hand, the entry forces the intermediate channel downward. Our conclusion at this point would be that the stock was headed lower, but that it would probably have a rally first.

At this point, however, the major channel has definitely turned upward, limiting our probable downside gains. We would be inclined to skip the short position and wait for the next good buy opportunity. There does not appear to be room for a very substantial drop before meeting the bottom line of the major channel.

Finally, let us look at the EMV figures (see Table 22-1), first using the plain 13-week crossover from plus to minus and minus to plus. We have a buy at week 32. This coincides with our other information telling us to buy there. The sell at week 57 is late, due to the narrowness of the prior top, but might reinforce our decision to stay short to week 64 instead of covering on week 58. The buy signal on week 67 is actually a bit early, since the stock is in a sideways area, but it would lead to a full participation in the subsequent advance. Obeying the plain 13-week crossover signals would have produced two break-evens and one very substantial profit, if taken alone.

Table 22–1
J. C. PENNEY

Weeks	13-Week ease of movement		Weeks	13-Week ease of movement		Weeks	13-Week ease of movement	
16	−48.2	Down	46	+27.1	Down	76	+22.5	Up
17	−44.4	Up	47	+42.9	Up	77	+38.6	Up
18	−33.4	Up	48	+36.7	Down	78	+37.0	Down
19	−31.3	Up	49	+32.5	Down	79	+43.1	Up
20	−12.1	Up	50	+19.7	Down	80	+22.4	Down
21	−19.7	Down	51	+19.5	Down	81	+13.8	Down
22	−15.1	Up	52	+ 9.2	Down	82	+25.1	Up
23	−21.9	Down	53	+ 5.4	Down	83	+33.4	Up
24	−29.2	Down	54	+ 5.0	Down	84	+65.4	Up
25	−36.7	Down	55	+ 3.0	Down	85	+69.3	Up
26	−33.0	Up	56	−0−	Down	86	+63.6	Down
27	−45.5	Down	57	− 9.4	Down	87	+85.7	Up
28	−55.5	Down	58	−13.1	Down	88	+97.0	Up
29	− 3.3	Up	59	−10.8	Up	89	+95.5	Down
30	− 5.6	Down	60	−16.8	Down	90	+75.8	Down
31	− 6.8	Down	61	−11.1	Up	91	+61.4	Down
32	+29.3	Up	62	− 9.6	Up	92	+67.0	Up
33	+29.8	Up	63	−15.6	Down	93	+54.4	Down
34	+44.3	Up	64	−21.1	Down	94	+15.1	Down
35	+47.0	Up	65	− 8.5	Up	95	−15.5	Down
36	+52.0	Up	66	− 8.8	Down			
37	+71.4	Up	67	+20.6	Up			
38	+80.4	Up	68	+33.7	Up			
39	+83.7	Up	69	+39.3	Up			
40	+89.0	Up	70	+43.7	Up			
41	+89.7	Up	71	+32.9	Down			
42	+47.1	Down	72	+27.3	Down			
43	+49.4	Up	73	+ 9.1	Down			
44	+58.4	Up	74	+13.9	Up			
45	+31.0	Down	75	+12.8	Down			

Used in conjunction with the other work, it would have helped somewhat as a confirming signal or an early warning.

Using, instead, only the 13-week figures when they give four-week reversals, we have somewhat better results. There would be a small profit from week 22 to week 54 on the long side. Weeks 51 to 70 would generate a good profit on the downside, and week 70 and on would generate another substantial profit on the upside. Combining them with the other work, they would be very helpful as early warnings. The buy at 22 appears 11 weeks before the stock turns strong. The sell at 51 comes in when we are still in the consolidation waiting for a signal, three weeks before the downside breakout. The buy at 70 implies the next move will be up, and is seen seven weeks before the dramatic upside move really begins. We believe that the combination of EMV figures with the other techniques provides the best approach to decision making, even though blindly following the EMV numbers has an excellent history.

Chapter 23   The Overall Market

It is certainly easier to make money on individual stocks when the overall market is going in the right direction. Consequently, one should always be aware of the wave patterns in the market and not try to fight dynamic market moves. If it is obviously a powerful bull market, there is no point in being short. Some stocks will be going down, but the majority will be in up cycles in phase with the market.

A bull market does not occur because stocks are more attractive on a fundamental basis; it occurs because people are willing to pay more for the same stocks. There is a general public move toward stocks, which pushes them higher. This change of attitude has an effect on most stocks, although there are always a few that are out of phase with the market. The important point is that shorting stocks in a strong bull market adds to the danger, as does buying stocks during a general market decline. Since we want as many factors as possible operating in our favor, there is no logic in trying to find the few strong stocks in a bear market or the few weak stocks in a bull market. As a general rule, if the overall market direction can be ascertained, never go against it.

In talking about the overall market direction, we do not mean the cycles that show up on the daily Dow charts (see Chapter 12), but rather the more important trends that are evident in the weekly or monthly charts. On the weekly charts (Figures 12–2 and 12–3), the major channel tells us the overall direction of the market. From February 1977 to March 1978, the market was obviously in a downmove, and, consequently, we should only have been looking for profitable shorts. After the turn upward in April 1978, it became obvious the major channel was pointed higher. During this phase only long positions should have been used.

There are times when the market is moving sideways—as in late 1976. Then there is no clear-cut direction. During such a phase, the trader should be equally ready to go long or short, depending upon the individual chart patterns.

Although we are deciding whether to use the long or the short side of stocks, based upon the major channel, we are not going to hold individual positions throughout the entire move. Consequently, we should also be aware of the smaller cycles enclosed by the major wave pattern. They can give us additional clues as to when moves are likely to begin or end in our individual issues. In long bull markets, most stocks do not advance throughout the entire market move; they take turns advancing. Market pullbacks are usually at points where one group of stocks stops moving and another group starts. Consequently, on market pullbacks we are likely to see an end to a move in the stocks we own, and should be looking for new opportunities.

The serious trader should keep market charts and be aware of the cycles. It can be very beneficial to his trading of the individual issues.

Chapter 24   The Trader's Checklist

The checklists on the following pages are designed to help the trader to analyze a stock, based upon the methods presented in this book. Use of such a checklist provides a discipline and helps to avoid emotional decisions.

Each question can be answered yes or no, with the yes answers being desirable. Inevitably, any stock will provide a few noes at any time, but each no should be carefully considered in making a decision. Too many no answers or noes to a few key questions may mean that it is not the right time to take a position on that stock.

The checklists are primarily aimed toward taking positions after a major consolidation. Often, however, good profits can be realized later in a move, after a secondary consolidation—a resting place on the way up or down. In this case, the lists can still be used and are just as effective.

There are two checklists—one for long positions, the other for short positions. We suggest making copies of these lists and filling one out before entering any position.

THE TRADER'S CHECKLIST—LONG POSITIONS

		Yes	No
1.	The stock:		
a.	Is it charted so boxes tell a readable story?	_____	_____
b.	Is there enough history?	_____	_____
c.	Is the stock liquid enough for easy trading?	_____	_____
d.	Does the stock show a good variety of box shapes?	_____	_____
e.	Does the stock have a history of big moves?	_____	_____
2.	The boxes:		
a.	Has it had any square or oversquare lows?	_____	_____
b.	Is movement easier to the upside?	_____	_____
c.	Has it had upside gaps?	_____	_____
d.	Does box shape get narrower across gaps?	_____	_____
3.	The patterns:		
a.	Has there been a consolidation?	_____	_____
b.	Has it broken out from the consolidation?	_____	_____
c.	Was it preceded by a long decline?	_____	_____
d.	Does the width of the consolidation justify a reasonable profit?	_____	_____
e.	Was the breakout a dramatic move?	_____	_____
f.	Has it penetrated the descending trendline?	_____	_____
g.	Are the lows ascending?	_____	_____
4.	Cycles:		
a.	Does the stock have reliable cycles?	_____	_____
b.	Is it near an expected low?	_____	_____
c.	Is the minor wave headed up?	_____	_____
d.	Is the minor wave near the bottom of its channel?	_____	_____
e.	Is the intermediate cycle headed up?	_____	_____
f.	Is the intermediate cycle near the bottom of its channel?	_____	_____
5.	EMV:		
a.	Has the EMV-13 gone positive?	_____	_____
b.	If not, is it likely to shortly?	_____	_____
c.	Has the EMV been reliable in the past?	_____	_____
6.	The market:		
a.	Is the market neutral or positive?	_____	_____
b.	Is the market near its cyclic low?	_____	_____
c.	Does this stock usually follow the market?	_____	_____
7.	Other considerations:		
a.	Are you acting solely on your technical work?	_____	_____
b.	Do you know at what price you would admit you were wrong?	_____	_____
c.	Do you know at what price you would take a profit?	_____	_____

THE TRADER'S CHECKLIST—SHORT POSITIONS

		Yes	No
1.	The stock:		
a.	Is it charted so boxes tell a readable story?	_____	_____
b.	Is there enough history?	_____	_____
c.	Is the stock liquid enough for easy trading?	_____	_____
d.	Does the stock show a good variety of box shapes?	_____	_____
e.	Does the stock have a history of big moves?	_____	_____
2.	The boxes:		
a.	Has it had any square or oversquare highs?	_____	_____
b.	Is movement easier to the downside?	_____	_____
c.	Has it had downside gaps?	_____	_____
d.	Does box shape get narrower across gaps?	_____	_____
3.	The patterns:		
a.	Has there been a consolidation?	_____	_____
b.	Has it broken out from the consolidation?	_____	_____
c.	Was it preceded by a long advance?	_____	_____
d.	Does the width of the consolidation justify a reasonable profit?	_____	_____
e.	Was the breakout a dramatic move?	_____	_____
f.	Has it penetrated the ascending trendline?	_____	_____
g.	Are the lows descending?	_____	_____
4.	Cycles:		
a.	Does the stock have reliable cycles?	_____	_____
b.	Is it near an expected high?	_____	_____
c.	Is the minor wave headed down?	_____	_____
d.	Is the minor wave near the top of its channel?	_____	_____
e.	Is the intermediate cycle headed down?	_____	_____
f.	Is the intermediate cycle near the top of its channel?	_____	_____
5.	EMV:		
a.	Has the EMV-13 gone negative?	_____	_____
b.	If not, is it likely to shortly?	_____	_____
c.	Has the EMV been reliable in the past?	_____	_____
6.	The market:		
a.	Is the market neutral or negative?	_____	_____
b.	Is the market near its cyclic high?	_____	_____
c.	Does this stock usually follow the market?	_____	_____
7.	Other considerations:		
a.	Are you acting solely on your technical work?	_____	_____
b.	Do you know at what price you would admit you were wrong?	_____	_____
c.	Do you know at what price you would take a profit?	_____	_____

Chapter 25   Conclusion

Now we have the discipline and the method. It is time to buy and sell stocks. Having heeded the advice of Chapter 20, we have separated ourselves from our emotions and are ready to approach the market in a businesslike manner. We are going to do our own work and expend the energy necessary to do a thorough analysis of the stock we are trading.

First, we must decide whether to keep daily or weekly charts, or both. This is largely a matter of time available and individual temperament. The most aggressive approach is to use daily charts and trade the swings within the intermediate channel, but many participants will not have the time to do this much work. Additionally, some are not able to make such rapid decisions. For these, weekly charts and longer-term trading are more suitable.

Second, how much money should be devoted to this type of activity? Again, it is an individual decision, based upon resources. The primary consideration should be the amount of money that a person can involve without upping his emotional stress to the point where he will make poor decisions. Do not trade with the grocery money!

To this point, we have assumed we are trading the stocks themselves, but what about options? This is a way of gaining very large leverage whereby a 10 percent move in the stock can easily become a 100 percent move in the underlying option. An aggressive trader should consider using options, but must be aware of the increased risks and must determine whether he is willing to assume that increased risk. If the leverage provided by the options increases his emotional involvement to the point where he cannot make detached, businesslike decisions, he should not be in the options market. If options are to be used, we suggest never buying an option with less than three months to expiration, and we prefer options which are close to strike price or slightly in the money. Buying an option which is about to expire introduces a pressure on the trader that may force him to make bad decisions. Buying an option which is way out of the money provides extremely high leverage, but we feel the risks are higher than necessary.

Should we use market orders or limit orders? In the underlying stocks of widely traded issues, market orders are no problem. If you want the stock, buy it and don't quibble over an eighth of a point. On thinly traded stocks and on options, we prefer limit orders as a protection against unhappy surprises. As before, however, if we have decided to buy the stock, let's buy it. The limit order should be placed at the last price or the asked side of the market. We are not trying to buy at a lower price, but we don't want to pay up unduly either.

Should we be willing to go short, or should we only play the long side of the market? Stocks move in both directions, and to limit ourselves to only long positions eliminates half the opportunities. A trader should be

137

just as willing to go short as to go long. Sometimes the overall market is in a slump, and going long makes no sense.

Should we use stop orders? A stop order provides an additional discipline, and some may find it necessary in order to avoid later rationalizations if the stock does not act right. We feel, however, that it is too automatic a system and prefer to watch each day's action, getting out when reason tells us to, rather than making decisions way in advance and backing those decisions with stop orders. Again, it is a question of the individual's ability to make unemotional decisions. A trader must, however, remember that he wants to be able to come back to fight again if he is wrong on a decision. This means preserving his buying power. Especially when one is trading options, wishful thinking can lead to such a depletion of assets that there is nothing left to use in a new situation. The smart trader will take an early loss, if necessary, but preserve enough of the money to move on to another opportunity.

The stock market is an exciting arena, where the smartest and best-prepared can triumph over the confused, lazy, or emotionally unprepared. We believe that luck plays almost no part in this battle. The victors are the gladiators who are most able.

Glossary

Bar Chart: Also called a vertical line chart. Price movement is depicted as a vertical line, its top being the highest price reached; its bottom, the lowest price reached.

Box Ratio (BR): The numerical value which represents the shape of an entry on an Equivolume chart. It is the volume divided by the range.

Breakout: A price move in a stock (or average) which moves it decisively out of a previously established consolidation area.

Breakaway Gap: A gap occurring as stock moves decisively out of a trading range. Typically, an increase in volume will accompany such a move.

Channel: A pair of parallel or nearly parallel lines which enclose the trading activity of a stock. They need not be straight lines.

Consolidation: A period during the trading history of a stock in which there is neither an advance nor a decline, and prices are restricted to a fairly narrow range.

Continuation Gap: A gap occurring during a strong advance or decline. Typically, volume and range are similar on both sides of the gap.

Cyclicality: A tendency for patterns to repeat. (See also *rhythm.*)

Ease of Movement Value (EMV): A numerical representation of the price movement of a stock, adjusted for price range and volume.

Exhaustion Gap: A gap that often occurs at the end of a significant series of price moves in one direction. Such a gap is typified by an increase in volume and a narrowing of the spread across the gap.

Float: That part of a company's outstanding stock which is actively traded in the marketplace.

Gap: A range of prices in which no trading occurs.

Intermediate Wave: In defining wave patterns using curvilinear channels, the second wave in the scaling-up process; larger than the minor wave and smaller than the major wave.

Major Wave: In defining wave patterns using curvilinear channels, the largest wave usually identified. The third wave in the scaling-up process. (See also *minor wave* and *intermediate wave.*)

Midpoint: The median price for a stock during a single day (or week) of trading (high + low $\div$ 2).

Midpoint Move: The difference between two consecutive midpoints, expressed as a positive or negative number.

Minor Wave: In defining wave patterns using curvilinear channels, the smallest wave.

Oversquare: An entry on an Equivolume chart which, due to the comparative range and volume, produces a rectangle wider than it is high.

Range: The high and low prices in a stock during a given day (or week) of trading.

Rectangular Consolidation: A sideways move in a stock, during which all of the lows occur at approximately the same price, as do all the highs.

Rhythm: Repetitive patterns that also have a regularity to the repetitions, usually assumed to be a time-based regularity.

Spread: The difference between the highest and lowest prices recorded in a stock during a given day (or week) (high − low = spread).

Square Entry: On an Equivolume chart, a day (or week) during which, due to the spread and volume, a rectangle is produced which has approximately equal horizontal and vertical dimensions.

Trend Line: A straight line on a chart that connects consecutive tops or consecutive bottoms.

Triangular Consolidation: A sideways move in a stock, during which tops and bottoms tend to converge rather than remain parallel, as in a rectangular consolidation.

Wave: Recurring high and low points that exhibit both cyclicality and rhythm.

Index

"The all-time heavyweight champion in the technical analysis field."

—*Stocks & Commodities Magazine, May 1994*

After ten years of developing investment software, we're still totally committed to just one thing—helping you become the best investor you can be.

That's why we add powerful new analysis methods like the Equivolume charting found in this book. In fact, MetaStock™ is the only program endorsed by Dick Arms, the developer of Equivolume charting.

As an EQUIS software user, you'll have access to a full range of help and support beyond the features you'll find in our programs.

When it comes to helping you become a successful computerized investor, we're here to help you every step of the way.

That's one of the reasons why MetaStock is the world's best-selling technical analysis software.

Here's what John Sweeney, Technical Editor at *Stocks & Commodities Magazine* discovered: "Most users I checked loved the relationship they had with EQUIS. Some had gotten unsolicited callbacks to see how they were doing. EQUIS was a company on which they could rely." (May 1994)

You can rely on us, too.

Order your FREE MetaStock Demo and a copy of *Maximizing Your Investments With MetaStock*, an information-packed booklet to help you get the most out of MetaStock.

Call Toll-Free:
1-800-882-3040 ext DA

Find out how MetaStock helps you become a successful investor.

See how you can become a successful computerized investor by ordering a free MetaStock Demo and booklet, *Maximizing Your Investments With MetaStock.*

You'll get a first-hand look at MetaStock, including the Equivolume charting you've seen in this book.

MetaStock™ is the world's best-selling technical analysis software. And it's the only program endorsed by Dick Arms, the developer of Equivolume charting.

Inside the booklet you'll find tips and ideas you can use with MetaStock to make better investment decisions:

- Get started with a Quick Tutorial
- Learn shortcuts, tips, and tricks

MetaStock lets you plot Equivolume and Candlevolume, plus more than 75 other built-in indicators and studies.

- Learn about compatible third-party products
- See how to use our free customer support network
- Learn about other MetaStock features
- Get special discounts on MetaStock and other EQUIS investment products

You'll see why the readers of *Stocks & Commodities Magazine* recently voted MetaStock #1 in its price category.

Investment software experts agree: "If you want to learn about technical analysis, this package is the place to start—and we guarantee that you'll never outgrow it. This may be the most well thought-out and easy-to-use package we reviewed."
—*Worth Magazine,* April 1994

With your own money on the line, you can trust MetaStock.

Order your FREE MetaStock Demo and a copy of *Maximizing Your Investments With MetaStock.*

Call Toll-Free:
1-800-882-3040 ext DA

EQUIS®
INTERNATIONAL

3950 South 700 East, Suite 100 · Salt Lake City, Utah 84107 · 801-265-8886 · FAX: 801-265-3999 · CompuServe: GO EQUIS (Section 14) Prodigy: Money Talk BB/Investment Tools/META   ©1994 EQUIS International, Inc. MetaStock is a trademark of EQUIS International. A real-time trading version of MetaStock is also available. Please call for more information.